Mary Baker Eddy: *The Golden Days*

"A Church in Scotland is dear to my heart, — it brings to memory the golden days of childhood, when Scotch tales were told at the fireside of my home."

... MARY BAKER EDDY
(from an unpublished letter)

Mary Baker Eddy: *The Golden Days*

By Jewel Spangler Smaus

Illustrated with photographs by Gordon Noble Converse

1966   **THE CHRISTIAN SCIENCE PUBLISHING SOCIETY**

Boston, Massachusetts, U.S.A.

All quotations in this book from *Retrospection and Introspection,* and from other writings, letters, and remarks of Mary Baker Eddy are used by permission of the Trustees under the Will of Mary Baker Eddy.

Quotations from *Mary Baker Eddy and the Stoughton Years,* Kenneth Hufford, and from many of the letters and other papers of the Baker family are used by permission of the Longyear Foundation, Brookline, Mass.

Grateful acknowledgement is made for permission to reprint selections from the following:

Child Life in New England, 1790-1840, Elizabeth George Speare; copyright © 1961, Old Sturbridge Village, Sturbridge, Mass.

The Cultural Life of the New Nation 1776-1830, Russel B. Nye; copyright © 1960, Harper & Row, Publishers, Incorporated, New York, N. Y.

History of American Congregationalism, Gaius Glenn Atkins and Frederick L. Fagley; copyright © 1942, The Pilgrim Press, Boston, Mass. Used by permission.

"Mary Baker Eddy, Discoverer and Founder of Christian Science: Her Life and Ancestry"; National Americana Society, Inc., New York, N. Y.

"Notes on Furnishing a Small New England Farmhouse" from *Old Time New England,* Vol. XLVIII; copyright © 1958, The Society for the Preservation of New England Antiquities, Inc., Boston, Mass.

Old Time Schools and School Books, Clifton Johnson; Dover Publications, Inc., New York, N. Y.

The Quimby Manuscripts, Horatio Dresser; copyright © 1961, The Julian Press, Inc., Publishers, New York, N. Y.

To my mother and my father and Kathryn B. Harrison,
who was my Sunday School teacher.

Foreword

Ten years of painstaking research have gone into the making of this book. It is written for young people, though it is hoped it will be of interest to all ages, since much of the material on which it is based has never before been examined.

Historical reconstruction has become a popular method for bringing history to life, and this is the presentation which I have used. Town histories, maps, almanacs, gazetteers, diaries, journals, paintings, photographs, artifacts — all these and more — have played their part.

Two years were spent with my family living in the town of Bow, New Hampshire, where Mary Baker was born and lived her childhood. Here the citizens, the town clerk, and selectmen were most generous in their assistance; similar help was found in the adjoining city of Concord, as well as in Pembroke, Sanbornton, and Tilton.

Old town records inaccessible before have finally been brought to light. My husband and two boys discovered forgotten landmarks, as they hiked the forests and meadows of Bow, retracing overgrown roads and paths used by the Baker family and their neighbors.

When we returned to our native California, there were additional years of research, during which many trips were made to New England, continuing the quest for material concerning Mary Baker and her family. I am particularly grateful to the residents of Sanbornton and Tilton who opened their memories as well as the attics of their homes during this period of historical reconstruction. Of special interest was the well-stuffed attic of the Sanbornton Town Hall where boxes of old records concerning Mark Baker and his family were found.

The resulting wealth of factual material has yielded an authentic story of the childhood and youth of Mary Baker — the golden days — a story that has never been told before.

With gratitude I acknowledge the generous assistance of the New Hampshire Historical Society, in Concord, New Hampshire. This organization formed well over a hundred years ago has much vital material relating to the Bakers and their period. Special thanks also must go to the Trustees of Longyear Foundation, in Brookline, Massachusetts, for granting unlimited access to the Foundation's priceless collection of Baker letters and papers, as well as personal possessions of the Baker family.

I am also deeply grateful to the Board of Trustees of The Christian Science Publishing Society for initiating and supporting the project and to The Christian Science Board of Directors for their constant encouragement and continuing interest. The Archives of The Mother Church have of course given invaluable assistance in the historical research.

It would be impossible in the limited space afforded here to thank all those individuals, from the East Coast to the West, who have given me assistance and encouragement. For my husband, who has helped me in so many ways during the past ten years, and my two sons; for the late Daisette D. S. McKenzie, one of Mrs. Eddy's students, who gave me a more profound understanding of Mary Baker Eddy's mission; for my teacher of Christian Science; for my sister and brother; for my secretary; for the editor, Allison W. Phinney, Jr., a grateful "thank you."

Finally, a wistful backward glance to the old Ordway-Richardson Farm, where my family and I found peaceful shelter during the two years of research in Bow. Forty-five acres of woods and fields, pond and stream, an old farmhouse and a sturdy barn, came as close to resembling the Baker homestead as can be managed these days, with modernization creeping over the Bow hills. When we left those hills for our native West, we knew well the meaning of the "golden days."

It has been a great joy for me to have come to know intimately during these past ten years Mary Baker, her mother and father, brothers and sisters, the Bow and Sanbornton years — as well as to trace the influence of these years in the momentous time that followed.

J.S.S.

Los Altos, California, June, 1966

Contents

Foreword 7

Illustrations 11

Prologue 13

The chapter titles are excerpts from Mary Baker Eddy's autobiography, *Retrospection and Introspection.*

Chapter 1 "In the Baker homestead at Bow I was born, the youngest of my parents' six children and the object of their tender solicitude." 15

Chapter 2 "My ancestors, according to the flesh, were from both Scotland and England. . . ." 18

Chapter 3 "My grandparents were likewise connected with Capt. John Lovewell of Dunstable, New Hampshire, whose gallant leadership and death, in the Indian troubles of 1722-1725, caused that prolonged contest to be known historically as Lovewell's War." 24

Chapter 4 "My childhood was also gladdened by one of my Grandmother Baker's books, printed in olden type and replete with the phraseology current in the seventeenth and eighteenth centuries." 28

Chapter 5 "Of my mother I cannot speak as I would, for memory recalls qualities to which the pen can never do justice." 34

Chapter 6 "My father possessed a strong intellect and an iron will." 40

Chapter 7 "Many peculiar circumstances and events connected with my childhood throng the chambers of memory." 45

Chapter 8 "Among the treasured reminiscences of my much respected parents, brothers, and sisters, is the memory of my second brother, Albert Baker, who was, next to my mother, the very dearest of my kindred." 50

Chapter 9 "From my very childhood I was impelled, by a hunger and thirst after divine things, — a desire for something higher and better than matter, and apart from it, — to seek diligently for the knowledge of God as the one great and ever-present relief from human woe." 56

Chapter 10 "In confidence of faith, I could say in David's words, 'I will go in the strength of the Lord God: I will make mention of Thy righteousness, even of Thine only. O God, Thou hast taught me from my youth: and hitherto have I declared Thy wondrous works.' (Psalms lxxi. 16, 17.)" 61

Chapter 11   "During my childhood my parents removed to Tilton, eighteen   **66**
miles from Concord, and there the family remained until the
names of both father and mother were inscribed on the stone
memorials in the Park Cemetery of that beautiful village."

Chapter 12   "My childhood's home I remember as one with the open hand."   **71**

Chapter 13   "My father was taught to believe that my brain was too large   **79**
for my body and so kept me much out of school, but I gained
book-knowledge with far less labor than is usually requisite."

Chapter 14   "My favorite studies were natural philosophy, logic, and moral   **88**
science."

Chapter 15   "The trend of human life was too eventful to leave me undis-   **94**
turbed in the illusion that this so-called life could be a real
and abiding rest."

Chapter 16   "In 1843 I was united to my first husband, Colonel George   **100**
Washington Glover of Charleston, South Carolina, the cere-
mony taking place under the paternal roof in Tilton."

Chapter 17   "After parting with the dear home circle I went with him [my   **107**
husband] to the South; but he was spared to me for only one
brief year. . . . A month later I returned to New Hampshire,
where, at the end of four months, my babe was born."

Chapter 18   "The night before my child was taken from me, I knelt by his   **116**
side throughout the dark hours, hoping for a vision of relief
from this trial."

Chapter 19   "My dominant thought in marrying again was to get back my   **123**
child, but after our marriage his stepfather was not willing he
should have a home with me."

Chapter 20   "All things earthly must ultimately yield to the irony of fate,   **130**
or else be merged into the one infinite Love."

Chapter 21   "When the door opened, I was waiting and watching...."   **138**

Chapter 22   "The miracles recorded in the Bible, which had before seemed   **144**
to me supernatural, grew divinely natural and apprehensible...."

Chapter 23   "Science and Health is the textbook of Christian Science."   **150**

Epilogue   **161**

Notes and Bibliography   **169**

Index   **189**

Illustrations

Mary Baker Eddy at Pleasant View, Concord, New Hampshire (June 1903),
    courtesy of the Archives of The First Church of Christ, Scientist,
    in Boston, Massachusetts;
    from a photograph taken by the Kimball studio, Concord   frontispiece

"The event was entered ... by the town clerk in his record book. ..."
    Old Town Hall, Bow, New Hampshire   facing page 16

"The four distinct New England seasons marked the passage of time
for the Bakers. ..."
    New Hampshire countryside   facing page 22

"These surefooted small-hooved animals were the chief beasts of
burden in the area."
    Old Sturbridge Village, Massachusetts   facing page 24

"As she grew older, she did expert needlepoint. ..."
    Madonna and child done by Mary Baker at the age of sixteen,
    courtesy Longyear Foundation, Brookline, Massachusetts.
    Background, the Farmhouse,
    Old Sturbridge Village, Massachusetts   facing page 30

"If Mr. Baker was not reading, he was working at his desk."
    Mark Baker's desk and personal possessions, including a sand
    shaker used for drying (blotting) the ink.
    Baker Room, Longyear Foundation   facing page 44

"The school term came to an end all too soon. ..."
    Original schoolhouse at Governor Dummer Academy,
    Newbury, Massachusetts   facing page 52

"She ... could only repeat what the Psalmist had declared. ..."
    Bible page   facing page 66

"She would often walk down to the river where it flowed past the
Baker property. ..."
    New Hampshire countryside   facing page 72

"... The elegance was temporary. In 1840 the carriage vanished
from the records. ..."
    Pleasure wagon, Old Sturbridge Village   facing page 86

"The Woodman Academy at the Square was a two-story building
beside the Congregational Church and the Town Hall."
    Now the town library at Sanbornton, New Hampshire   facing page 92

". . . words are impotent things to utter the feelings of a Mother's heart."
    The Farmhouse, Old Sturbridge Village   facing page 122

"The house was near the main road beside a mountain stream."
    *Groton House, North Groton, New Hampshire,
    maintained by the Longyear Foundation*   facing page 128

". . . she attended the Congregational Church that stood on a hill
overlooking the village of North Groton."
    Maintained by the Longyear Foundation   facing page 130

"In the small room so close to the stars, Mary Baker Glover
finished her book."
    *Lynn Historical House, Lynn, Massachusetts,
    maintained by the Christian Science Church*   facing page 160

Prologue

Mary Baker Eddy stepped lightly from her study onto the balcony. As she looked down upon the crowd gathered in the gardens below, only her white hair gave a clue to her more than eighty years.

It was June, 1903.[1] There were almost ten thousand men, women, and children standing quietly in the gardens and in the road, their faces upturned to greet the woman who had discovered and founded Christian Science, the greatly loved author of the book called *Science and Health with Key to the Scriptures.* Mrs. Eddy had stated, "They who know (understand) my book know me." [2] Many of those present felt they knew her well, for in a time of need they had read her book and had been healed of serious diseases. Some had found a new way of life, release not only from pain but from sin and grief.

They had come, these thousands, to meet her at her home in Concord, New Hampshire. From all parts of the United States and the world they had traveled first to Boston, Massachusetts, to attend the Annual Meeting of the Christian Science Church. Then, at the invitation of Mrs. Eddy, they had come by special trains to the city of Concord. It was a rare treat for these Christian Scientists. Years before, Mrs. Eddy had retired from the public eye to revise *Science and Health* and to give more time to prayer. This gathering was one of her few public appearances. She did not want flattering admiration or a worshipful attitude from the members of the church she had founded. Her effort had been to build a strong church government that would not require her to be present personally to carry on its affairs.

But she did love these people. As she looked out at the thousands of faces — children standing quietly, some women waving their handkerchiefs in silent greeting, men bareheaded — she lifted her hands out towards them as if to take each one to her heart. A radiant smile lighted her face as she spoke briefly. Her voice was strong and vibrant. There was not a sound from that vast audience.

Beyond the crowd, beyond the gardens and the valley, rose the hills of Bow. Often Mrs. Eddy's eyes had rested lovingly on those distant hills, and often, as she sat at work in her study, she had thought of the old farmhouse that once stood on a knoll in line with her study windows.

In a small book telling of her life and her inner thoughts, a book she called *Retrospection and Introspection,* Mary Baker Eddy had told of the farm and the "golden days" of her childhood. Simply and briefly she had shared with those who longed to know her the story of her life and of her discovery of Christian Science. . . .

1

*"In the Baker homestead at Bow I was born, the youngest of my
parents' six children and the object of their tender solicitude."*
... Retrospection and Introspection
MARY BAKER EDDY

High on a hill in Bow, New Hampshire, the Baker homestead looked
down on the Londonderry Turnpike. From the front doorstep swirls of
dust could be seen marking the narrow dirt road where the stagecoach
from Boston clattered by.

Below the turnpike, on the broad Merrimack River, a flat-bottomed
boat with a single square sail glided upstream toward the Bow Canal
and Concord, the capital of New Hampshire.

Monday, July 16, 1821, was a warm summer day.[1] A westerly breeze
stirred yellow goldenrod unfurling along the stone walls of the Baker
farm. Blueberries ripened in the sunny fields. The wind brought the
sound of the steady rasp of a sawmill across the hills.

In the fields the men swung scythes, and boys raked hay into stacks,
making it ready for the hay racks. July had been a warm, wet month—
good growing weather. There had been heavy rain, so that the grass had
been too wet for mowing, but now for several days there had been clear
skies. The weather had made it possible for the Bakers to work in the
fields on Friday and Saturday. No work had been done on Sunday,
although Mark Baker was doubtless anxious to continue the harvesting
before the dry spell ended. Only the most necessary work, such as
feeding the farm animals, was ever done on the Sabbath.

There were two barns on the Baker property, a large one separate
from the house and a smaller one connected to the house by a series of
sheds.[2] Both were to be filled with hay for the winter, and Samuel,
Albert, and George, like most farm children, were expected to help. The
boys were only thirteen, eleven, and eight, but they often did what in
later years would be considered the job of grown men. Haying was
important work, providing food for the animals during the long New

England winter that lay ahead. Mark Baker had recently purchased additional fields in Concord to assure an adequate supply.

But on this warm Monday in July thoughts were not entirely on the haying season. There was unusual excitement and expectation at the Baker house. For days the "best" room had been ready for the arrival of a new baby.

When the good news came, Mark and his three boys came in from the fields. They all crowded into the room, along with Grandmother Maryann Baker and the two little sisters, five-year-old Abby and two-year-old Martha. Now there were an even half-dozen Baker children — three boys and three girls.

The event was entered dryly and factually by the town clerk in his record book, the last entry for the Baker family:

Mr. Mark Baker   Abigail his Wife
their Children Born as followeth
Samuel Dow Baker Born July 8th 1808
Albert Baker Born February 5th 1810
George Sullivan Baker Born August 7th 1812
Abigail Barnard Baker Born Jany 15th 1816
Martha Smith Baker Born Jany 19th 1819
Mary Morse Baker Born July 16th 1821.

Sally Gault, a neighbor and Abigail Baker's closest friend, was perhaps one of the first to see the newest child. Andrew Gault and Mark Baker served together on several town committees, and the children of the two families were about the same age. A well-worn path ran between their neighboring woods and apple orchards.[3]

Sally Gault had a special interest in this child. In the months before Mary was born, she had walked up the path through the orchard many times to pray with her friend.[4] The two women often read the Bible and prayed aloud together. This was not an uncommon practice, for at that time in New England thoughts of God were very much a part of everyday life. Like their neighbors, the Bakers devoted the entire Sunday to

"The event was entered . . . by the town clerk in his record book. . . ."
Old Town Hall, Bow, New Hampshire

the worship of God. They attended Sunday services, morning and afternoon, at the old Meeting House on White Rock Hill, and throughout the week they held daily family prayers in the morning and evening.

In personal letters, conversation, books, and newspapers of that day such phrases as the "rich mercies of Christ," the "salvation of the Lord," and the "will of God" were frequent. In one early history of New England, a chapter was titled "Remarkable Answers to Prayer." Whatever happened to these devout people was considered the will of God. If it was good, God gave it. If it was bad, they believed it was also God's will for His children, who must be made to learn that they were "as nothing before His fearsome Presence."

Abigail Baker would obediently humble herself before her Creator as a "sinful mortal," but she felt nevertheless that she understood Him best as a loving God and she guided her children to look upon Him in this way. Such thoughts of God contrasted with the religious doctrines of her church, which emphasized fear of the Lord, the sinful nature of man, and the dread punishments said to be awaiting each mortal sinner in the afterworld. Mark Baker, for his part, held rigidly to a fearsome view of impending punishment by an unmercifully stern God.

Like most mothers, Abigail felt certain that all her children were unusual and talented. They were, in fact, bright youngsters, and each expressed a strong individuality. Of Mary, in particular, Abigail could not help expecting great things.

Even before Mary's birth Abigail had shared with her friend Sally Gault a unique conviction about the child. Abigail had told Sally how one day she climbed the narrow stairs to the attic in the Baker home to get a fresh supply of wool for spinning. The room was only dimly lighted by small windows, as the back roof sloped in the fashion of the saltbox house, straight from the ridgepole to one story above the kitchen. In the soft light of the attic room, hung with fragrant herbs, Abigail's thought was at peace. Gathering up the wool in this quiet place, she was suddenly filled with an unusual consciousness of God's goodness and power. She felt released from everyday concerns and saw something of the meaning of the "dominion" spoken of in Scriptural passages which were often in her thought. It was a sacred and exalting experience.

But when the moment of inspiration had passed, Abigail told Sally that she had been stricken with guilt. Raised in the Calvinistic doctrine that man is only a miserable sinner and able to comprehend little of God's glory, she felt wicked to have entertained such thoughts. And yet, she told Sally, she could not keep herself from the conviction that the expected child was set apart by God. The two women talked it over often, praying together, and asking God's guidance.

Sally Gault was undoubtedly thinking of all this as she entered the "best" room. As her eyes met Abigail's, she must have wondered about this child and about the mother's conviction — wondered what kind of life lay ahead for Mary Baker.

2

"My ancestors, according to the flesh, were from both Scotland and England. . . ."

... *Retrospection and Introspection*
MARY BAKER EDDY

The year 1821 slipped into autumn, and the scent of ripening wild grapes filled the air. Wild asters purpled in the fields, and along stone walls the goldenrod blossomed into feathery plumes.

The sun was still warm during the day, but at night there was a touch of frost in the air. The Bakers began to prepare for winter. Grandmother Baker sat often by the fire, rocking the baby beside her in the cradle. For her, the fall round of activities was familiar and reassuring. She had settled the land with her husband, Joseph, long before the Revolutionary War. When Mark, the youngest of the ten children, married, he had brought his bride to the farm and stayed on with his father as the older brothers left.[1] To the west, on the Baker road and the next hill over, James Baker had built a farmhouse, and Philip had settled toward the east, nearer the river.

Even before his father's death, Mark had taken over much of the management of the homestead. Now, like his Bow neighbors, he was providing against the winter as he had for many years. Sheds were to be filled with wood, roofs repaired, and the foundation of the farmhouse banked with brush and evergreens for insulation. There were apples to be harvested and cider to be made at Andrew Gault's cider mill. There the juice flowed temptingly in a steady amber stream, and at one pressing as many as twenty-six barrels were filled to be stored in the Bakers' cool cellar.[2]

The earthen-floored cellar also held bins and barrels of apples, potatoes, onions, beets, squashes, cabbages, as well as salted pork and dried salmon from the Merrimack. There was good fishing in the river. In a few hours one day, a Bow neighbor had caught six salmon, a catch weighing eighty pounds.[3]

Abigail went about the unending tasks of the New England house-wife — cooking in the great open fireplace, washing, cleaning, spinning, weaving, sewing, making gallons of soap and dozens of candles, churning butter, and pressing cheese. In the fall she added to her work the preserving of food for winter. She dried apples, herbs, and berries. She cooked apple sauce and apple butter outdoors in a huge copper kettle.

Even small children like five-year-old Abby were expected to help with the chores. Abby showed a talent for orderliness and the ability to take responsibility at an early age. In temperament she seemed more like her father than her mother. Among other tasks, Abby was probably expected to dip water from the well and the rain barrel. Martha, of course, was much too young to be depended upon. She helped her mother best by keeping out from underfoot and amusing her baby sister, Mary.

When the children were not kept busy around the house they visited a rocky ledge known as "the playground." It extended along the lower part of the Baker hill overlooking the turnpike and was a natural grandstand for watching the road. In autumn, stagecoaches and wagons rolled along under a canopy of red and gold leaves — oak, beech, and maple shimmering in the brilliant sunlight. Sometimes an eight-horse freight wagon rumbled by. It was as exciting to the children as catching a glimpse of the Boston stage.[4]

The farm commanded a sweeping view of distant hills. The colorful autumn pageant continued for days, and during the fall rains, the foliage took on an even brighter, luminous glow against the dark sky. Just before Thanksgiving, when the leaves were gone and the branches stark, the first light snowfall covered the hills.

A few days before Christmas there was a heavy snow which afforded good sleighing. The Bakers, wrapped snugly in buffalo robes, with hot stones at their feet, skimmed over the snow in the horse-drawn sleigh. The long string of jingling harness bells echoed in the crisp air.

Travel was swift on the snowpacked turnpike. With less outside work to be done at the farm, the Bakers enjoyed frequent visits to the state capital, only a few miles away. Mark's brother Philip and his sister Mary Ann had married into the prominent Dow family of Concord, and there were Abigail's uncle and two cousins on the Ambrose side.[5] This branch of the Ambrose family was particularly well known in Concord, active in both church and town affairs.

The capital was a lively place. A number of stage lines entered the city, and nearly all travel from northern Vermont and New Hampshire converged on Concord. As the girls grew up, they had no problem keeping in step with the latest fashions, while Mark Baker and the boys could keep abreast of politics. Westward expansion of the young country brought exciting news nearly every day. Just the year before, in 1820,

Maine had been admitted as a free state. Then, in 1821, Missouri was admitted as a slaveholding state, making twenty-four states in all. It was President James Monroe's second term.

The state legislature met in the capitol building, topped with an impressive dome and gilt eagle. Newly enacted laws of the nation were published in full on the front page of one of Concord's newspapers, the *Daily Patriot,* and local politics were given extensive coverage.

There were a number of fine, large hotels in the city. Main Street bustled with wagons carrying goods freighted up the Merrimack River by canal boat. Brightly painted stagecoaches set off for distant points. Advertisements in the papers boasted of the latest fashions from Boston and Paris for both men and women. There was notice of "ladies French habit cloths in fashionable colors, elegant millinery, and satin slippers." For the men, the Concord Emporium advertised the "latest and most prevailing fashions: vests, pantaloons, and trimmings."

There was no letup in the smooth flow of traffic on the turnpike past the Baker homestead into Concord. Farmers saved heavy hauling for winter, and all day long pungs or country sleds glided along, laden with butter, cheese, and dried apples for city markets. The driver, managing his horses from a perch at the back, usually wore a buffalo coat and fox-skin cap, the long tail whipping back and forth behind him in the wind.

During blizzards, few ventured out. The wind blew the snow in great drifts across roads and paths, against the stone walls and around the corners of the houses and sheds. Farm animals were bedded down in the barn adjoining the house, so that at feeding time Mark and the boys could go through the sheds without setting foot outside.

When a blizzard subsided, the children tumbled outdoors. Snow forts appeared and snowballs flew through the crisp air. When ponds had been cleared, there was ice skating. The river had iced over in December that year, and it was not until March of 1822 that boats began to move again.

Early spring was sugaring time. Small holes were drilled into the maple trees and into each hole a wooden spout was driven. From these the sweet tree sap dripped all day long into buckets. The thin liquid was periodically collected and boiled until it turned to heavy syrup — or if boiled longer, to maple sugar.

The Baker children celebrated the close of the sap season with sugaring-off parties. Hot syrup was poured over servings of snow to make maple candy. A pan of maple sugar was set out in the hall for visitors, and a large pitcher of syrup was provided to pour out for tasting.

When spring comes to New England, it arrives quickly in a burst of color and fragrance. In May of 1822, the apple orchards were in bloom, the blossoms especially full this spring. First of the flowers in the forest and meadows was the trailing arbutus, or mayflower, its fragrant pink and white blooms half hidden under beds of dry leaves and pine needles. Where the brook tumbled through the woods between banks of moss and fern, purple violets and bright yellow cowslips spread carpets of color. Wild cherry blossoms made lacework against the fresh green of new birch leaves and the darker green of the pines. Purple and white lilac bloomed in the dooryard.

By Mary's first birthday, in July, her father and the boys were again busy with haying. The four distinct New England seasons marked the passage of time for the Bakers, and to a great extent they lived with the rhythm of planting and harvest.

In the spring of 1825 she was almost four, with chestnut brown curly hair that framed rosy cheeks and blue eyes. The blue eyes could become dark and spark with righteous indignation when she felt some wrong was done. She was not often angry except over injustice. But even then, although ready to fly into the midst of a fray, she was quick to forgive and forget when the wrong had been corrected.[6]

An active and mischievous child, Mary was beginning to show signs of a capacity for periods of quiet thoughtfulness. She was a sensitive

"The four distinct New England seasons marked the passage of time
for the Bakers. . . ."
New Hampshire countryside

youngster and seemed to her parents more frail than any of the other children.

She had a good sense of fun, as did her pretty sister Martha and red-headed George. Hide-the-thimble and hide-and-seek were favorite games, and Mary was particularly good at both of them.

As the youngest, she was well loved by the family, who took care to include her in family activities. But from the beginning she enjoyed quiet times by herself. She would sit for hours in her small rocking chair, looking at the Bible as she had seen her mother and grandmother do.

She learned to read early, perhaps because of family Bible reading and the assistance of her older sisters and brothers. Albert, who was the acknowledged student of the family, was especially helpful. Though he was fifteen and Mary only four, there seemed to be a closer bond between them than between the other children.

Mary was a happy child and liked to be outdoors roaming the fields and pastures. She loved the farm animals and was especially fond of Hunt, her father's Newfoundland dog.

Mark Baker always kept at least ten oxen.' These surefooted, small-hooved animals were the chief beasts of burden in the area. A big pair might weigh as much as twenty-eight hundred pounds, but could weave nimbly around rocks and trees while pulling extremely heavy loads. In addition, there were usually four or five cows, five horses, and chickens, pigs, and sheep. Most Bow farms had similar livestock.

Mary liked to ride horseback, and she was gentle and adept with the farm animals. Her father sometimes let her care for sickly young lambs. "Here is another invalid for Mary," he would say when he brought in some weakling from the flock and, before long, Mary would have patiently nursed it back to health.

Like many children, she loved to listen to her grandmother's stories, often tales of her Scottish and English ancestors. The family was descended from the McNeils, originally of Scotland. Grandmother Maryann

Baker was proud to be a cousin of the hero General John McNeil, who had led the bayonet charge at the battle of Chippewa in the War of 1812.

America was still young, and family stories were often accounts of pioneer life as full of adventure as any novel. Only a few years after the Pilgrims had landed at Plymouth the first Baker had emigrated to New England to escape religious persecution. He made the passage in a small sailing vessel and brought with him only the essentials for living. Everyday belongings were so precious that Thankful Baker, one of Mary's ancestors, considered her best kettle and best bed important enough to be listed in the family's inheritance.[8]

Thomas Baker, the first of Mary Baker's own forebears to emigrate from England to America, had come to Roxbury, Massachusetts, in 1640. At that time, the hilltop in Bow was still part of the unexplored wilderness, and most of New England was a vast forest of towering pines and gigantic oaks.

To Mary, the most exciting stories her grandmother told were of her great-grandparents and the Indians.

3

"My grandparents were likewise connected with Capt. John Lovewell of Dunstable, New Hampshire, whose gallant leadership and death, in the Indian troubles of 1722–1725, caused that prolonged contest to be known historically as Lovewell's War."

... Retrospection and Introspection
MARY BAKER EDDY

For some years settlers had stayed close to the coast of New England, near ports and fishing villages. Gradually, traders and trappers followed Indian paths and made their way inland.

In 1638 a scouting party explored and mapped the Merrimack River, discovering in the Bow area three large waterfalls where salmon fishing was especially good. The Penacook tribe was settled on the banks of the

"These surefooted small-hooved animals were the chief beasts of burden in the area."
    Old Sturbridge Village, Massachusetts

river. Indians in New Hampshire at that time did not usually attack settlers openly, but they would make sudden raids for the purpose of taking captives which they sold for bounty to the French in Canada.

Maryann Baker,¹ Mary's grandmother, told stories of small pioneer groups that followed scouting parties and settled along the river in spite of such dangers. One of these pioneers was Mary's great-grandfather, Captain Joseph Baker. Dates and intricate family genealogy were hard for the Baker children to follow. But history was vivid enough in stories of great-grandfather Joseph's brushes with the Indians and the hardships the family endured!

Born near Boston in 1714, Captain Joseph Baker came to Bow with a party of early settlers when only a youth. First a cart path had been hewn through the forest, then clearings made among the tall pines. As Captain Baker and other settlers went about the task of clearing land, building houses and barns, and growing crops, they were always on the alert for Indians.

Mary's grandmother remembered the story of an Indian battle fought on the banks of the Merrimack. It may have been the arrowheads from this battle that the Baker children and their friends found when the water along the river bank was low.

In the spring of 1747, the Indians made a number of attacks about the countryside. A Bow farmer was killed, and another farmer and his ten-year-old son captured, though they escaped some time later. Captain Joseph Baker worked with his gun close at hand and was ready to join in defending the town whenever there was an Indian alarm. He was head of a Company of Foot during the French and Indian War.

In 1739, Captain Baker married the daughter of Captain John Lovewell, the famous Indian fighter. Lovewell and most of his men had lost their lives in a heroic stand against the Indians. History books took note of it as Lovewell's War, and a favorite ballad of the day included the stanza:

Of worthy Captain Lovewell I purpose now to sing,
How valiantly he served his country and his king;
He and his valiant soldiers did range the woods full wide,
And hardships they endured to quell the Indians' pride.[2]

A large grant of land was given to the "survivors and heirs of the deceased soldiers of Captain Lovewell's expedition." This grant later became the towns of Pembroke and Bow.

Hannah Lovewell Baker possessed the courage of her famous father. Her story has been told and retold, and was probably related by Mary's grandmother very much as it is given in the *History of Pembroke*.[3]

Hannah Baker was washing her clothes one day by a spring during the Indian troubles of 1747, when an alarm was sounded indicating the presence of Indians in the neighborhood. It was a signal for all to get quickly to the nearest garrison house. However, Hannah was almost finished with her washing, and she intended to see it completed. Even though her husband and a neighbor pleaded with her to accompany them to safety, she refused. As soon as the men reached the fort, they formed a rescue party and went back to save Hannah, only to meet her as she walked to the garrison in a leisurely manner, carrying the basket of clothes washed to her complete satisfaction.

The story of her life became a legend. It was her son Joseph who was to marry Maryann, Mary's grandmother. The newlyweds moved across the Merrimack River to the west side and pioneered the old homestead that was to be Mary Baker's birthplace. This land was part of the original Lovewell grant. At first, both sides of the Merrimack River in this area were named Bow, but later the east side was divided into several towns, among them Pembroke.

By the time Joseph and Maryann Baker settled on the west side, there was no longer danger of Indian attack. However, as pioneers of the town of Bow, they showed the same courage and resolution as had the earlier Bakers. They, too, carved their home from the land, cutting the virgin forest, clearing the fields, and building stone walls. Joseph planted an apple orchard and peach trees, pears, and cherries.

He had a part in establishing the town — the Meeting House on White Rock Hill, the schools, and the roads. He was one of a committee chosen to locate the exact Bow Center.

Joseph Baker held a succession of town offices. At one time he was a selectman, one of the most important positions in a New England town. The selectmen made up the chief governing body and were elected by the townspeople at annual meeting when male citizens gathered to vote on all matters of local government.

At this time, America was still an English colony. But rumblings of discontent with what were considered unfair laws and taxes imposed by England were being heard even in Bow. They were echoed in the Town Book of Records.[4] In 1775, citizens voted at a town meeting "to raise money to buy a . . . stock of ammunition," although Bow was then a town of only three hundred and fifty people.

Hardy, independent settlers like these Bow townspeople were used to taking care of themselves. They supported their government, but a man who worked with his gun by his side, who had the courage to fight off marauding Indians, was not one to look lightly on what he felt were unjust laws.

When the growing discontent exploded in America, the farmers at Lexington took up arms and Paul Revere made his famous ride. The town of Bow was ready. Men from Bow fought at Lexington, Bennington, and Ticonderoga, and New Hampshire was proudly represented throughout the Revolutionary War.[5]

During the war years, Joseph served on the Bow Committee of Safety. The town was hard pressed to raise money to equip and send soldiers to the battlefronts, and for several years money for schooling and preaching was spent for war instead.

In 1785, four years before George Washington took office as President of the new United States, Mary's father, Mark, was born. When he had grown to manhood, Mark took a strong interest in town affairs, as had his father. The year he was married, in 1807, he held his first office as surveyor of highways for the town of Bow. The work called for the planning and construction of roads and bridges. With maturity, Mark became as well known in town activities as his father, Joseph, and his grandfather, Captain Joseph, before him.

4

"My childhood was also gladdened by one of my Grandmother Baker's books, printed in olden type and replete with the phraseology current in the seventeenth and eighteenth centuries."

...Retrospection and Introspection
MARY BAKER EDDY

Mark Baker's interests often ranged beyond the town of Bow to affairs of the county and state. Guests in the Baker home were apt to carry on long discussions of government, religion, and politics. Mary frequently listened or overheard, and quietly she was forming her own opinions about religion.

The kitchen-family room, with its large fireplace, was the gathering place for the Bakers.[1] In later years Mary referred nostalgically to the sturdy old table that was used by the children for study and letter writing. The rhythmic tick of a tall grandfather calendar clock echoed through the room. The case, which was almost as high as the ceiling, was made of gleaming mahogany, the face of brass. As the long pendulum swung back and forth, the clock marked off the days of the month as well as the hours and minutes. It was one of the Bakers' prized possessions, made by a famous clockmaker in Concord.[2]

In the evenings Abigail Baker, usually occupied with mending or sewing, sat in a low rocking chair. Mary perched on a footstool or drew up her own small rocker, while Grandmother kept at her knitting. She was never far from it, for her needles were always pinned to a shield on the side of her skirt.[3]

Candles held in floor stands cast a flickering glow, and a pewter whale-oil lamp brightened the dark corners.[4] The fireside was the center of activity in an early American home — a snug retreat on a winter night, as well as a family forum. There was lively talk about the happenings of the day, and the younger children were entertained with stories.

Nearly everyone was busy in the evening with handiwork, since many clothes, linens, and utensils were made rather than bought. The older girls did needlework, and Mary was learning already from her mother and her sisters. As she grew older, she did expert needlepoint, beadwork, and sewing.[5] The boys might be hammering out square iron nails on a bench equipped with a small anvil. It was a good way to earn money in the winter, providing a trickle of credit at Mr. Clough's general store at Bow Center.

Mark Baker often read, or he might be at his desk drawing up a will.[6] He sometimes acted as a lawyer for his neighbors and the town of Bow. He was town agent in lawsuits against Loudon and Hooksett and represented Bow in the Court of Common Pleas in Concord. He was not a learned man and had only the education afforded by a one-room school, but by nature he seemed more suited to a profession such as law or the ministry than to farming. He enjoyed nothing better than a long, theological discussion with a clergyman.

For many years he was county coroner, representing the town of Bow.[7] As such, it was his duty to conduct an official inquiry before a jury when there was reason to suppose that any death in the town was due to unnatural causes.

Mark was a good enough farmer, but had no special talent for it. Along with the usual crop of hay, he raised wheat, corn, oats, rye, and vegetables.[8] He managed to break even each year, and the farm provided for his family's needs a little more adequately than in the case of some neighbors.

Those who had a talent other than farming sometimes had small shops at their homes — a blacksmith shop, a gun shop, a shoemaker's shop, as did Uncle Philip, or a mill, as did Uncle James's son Luke. Mark Baker's shop was his desk.

The Bakers were a hospitable family. They often took in a traveling clergyman for the night or boarded a district schoolteacher. As one of the family once remarked, they were "partial to that class of people." [9]

Mark Baker was well informed, and his wife had a talent for keeping the conversation "pleasing and profitable," in the words of a minister who often visited the family.

Broad opinions on all subjects were freely expressed and occasionally hotly disputed. Mark could be outspoken and strong-willed. His children showed something of his forceful, independent spirit. Samuel, at eighteen, was already planning to leave home to learn the building trade in Boston. Albert was determined to read and study every spare moment he could find. Nearly sixteen, he was tall and dark-haired, with a high forehead and brown eyes. He had decided he would not take up farming but would be a lawyer.

Albert was an exceptionally bright student and was planning to teach school in Concord during the academic year of 1826 to earn money to continue his own education. Mark Baker could spare little, with six children to support and only a small cash income. The school was #18 of the Iron Works District adjoining Bow. Typical of the period — according to Concord records — it had one room eighteen by twenty feet, with a low ceiling and a stone fireplace. The young man would be paid $3.35 a month, and would have thirty-two pupils of all ages in these cramped quarters. [10]

Albert alternated periods of teaching with his own attendance at
high school, a private school across the river called Pembroke

Academy. Towns and cities provided free schooling only through the elementary grades, and very few young people could afford further education.

Albert boarded with Mark's good friend, the Reverend Abraham Burnham, the Congregational minister for Pembroke. Mr. Burnham was a vigorous, warmhearted man, largely responsible for the establishment and success of Pembroke Academy. He had once been a hired farm boy, but through his own efforts had gone on to Dartmouth College and graduated with honors. He helped many boys to set out on the path toward a college education.[11]

Mary's older sisters, Abby and Martha, liked to read and enjoyed their schoolwork. Later Martha wrote delightful, witty letters, Abby and Mary a little more serious compositions. George had a certain flair for spinning dramatic tales, and could dash off a poem on a moment's notice. When Mary was older, George sometimes exchanged verses with her.[12] He was round-faced and full of fun, impetuous and generous. He was quick to show both love and anger.

Mark Baker could sympathize with Albert's desire to be a lawyer, but George's creative ability did not fit any pattern familiar to him. Mark, as Joseph Baker's youngest son, had stayed on with his father, and it seemed to him that his own youngest son should plan to stay on the farm.

All the Baker children did some reading outside school because there were always books at home. Their parents were well read for their day, although books were comparatively rare and expensive. Printing was just becoming an important industry. There were now shops in Concord where books were printed and bound; and small pocket-size volumes, in soft, brown leather or in hard paper, were shared eagerly with good friends.

Mary's grandmother had a number of books that she and her husband had gathered over the years. One old school book had been inscribed by Mark, Uncle Philip, and a neighbor, as was the custom when a book was handed down from pupil to pupil. This particular volume had been published in 1796 and had the unending title, *An American Selection of Lessons in Reading and Speaking Calculated to Improve the Minds and Refine the Taste of Youth and also to Instruct Them in the Geography, History and Politics of the United States!*

At an early age, Mary learned to love books. The large family Bible and her own smaller edition were her favorites. She undoubtedly learned her first sentences from them. The Psalms and the stories of Jesus' healings of the sick were among her favorites when she learned to read for herself.

Her grandmother's books were kept in a chest in the attic, along with an ancient rusted sword in a brass scabbard, a family heirloom from Scotland, nearly five hundred years old. Just as interesting to the child was a yellowed handwritten manuscript composed by Maryann Baker's mother, containing sonnets on the Scriptures, and other verses.

When she was quite young, Mary became acquainted with school books. It was not unusual for the younger children in a family to be taken to school during a short summer session, sometimes called dame's school because it was taught by a woman. During the winter session, school was too crowded for the youngest. But during the summer months the older boys were at work on the farm, and the girls and the younger boys attended. Busy farm mothers were happy to be able to pack a lunch for the little ones and send them off for the day with their older sisters.

Schooling was now ordered by state law in New Hampshire. Each town was required to support adequate schoolhouses and teaching. In these early years in America, "adequate" usually meant just that, only the fundamentals of learning — reading, writing, and arithmetic. Embellishments were added at the discretion of the teacher and according to the caliber of the local school committee.

There were seven one-room schoolhouses in Bow, New Hampshire. The Baker children attended School #3, at the junction of the Londonderry Turnpike and the old county road, just a mile from their home.[13]

One summer day in 1826, Abby, who was ten years old, Martha, seven, and Mary, nearly five, started down the path through the orchard. It was to be Mary's first day at school.

The girls, who looked very much alike, were also dressed alike, in frocks, made by their mother. Everyday school dresses made of cloth woven at home were fashioned with sleeves puffed at the shoulder, simple necklines, and full skirts that fell almost to the ankles. Peeking out from the edge of the skirts were stiff, starched pantalets.

The Baker girls may have stopped for Matthew Gault. He was just Martha's age, and still too young to work in the fields. Matthew was dressed in homespun shirt and trousers, and went barefoot in the summer. He had one pair of shoes, made of tough cowhide, which was to last a year.

Schoolhouse #3 had been built a few years before according to plans drawn up by Mark Baker, who was always active on the school committee during his residence in Bow.

Country schools were simple buildings, often constructed on land given for the purpose because it was not good enough for anything else. School #3 was only twenty-two feet square, with a low ceiling and small-paned windows. The walls were whitewashed plaster, without any sort of decoration or color. The main concerns of the school committee were the continual repair of broken windowpanes and the never-ending problem of obtaining wood for the fireplace. Mark Baker often supplied the wood and repaired the windows.

The schoolmistress sat at an elevated desk in order to be well above the level of the children's narrow tables and benches. With eight grades in one classroom, it was necessary to keep a sharp eye for mischief and wandering attention. Summer school was easier to teach than the winter session because there were no older boys. The children worked with slates and slate pencils brought from home. For the most part, they used whatever books the family owned or could borrow.

On this first day in school, Mary Baker sat in the front row on the middle bench, which was lower than the others so that younger children could sit with their feet touching the floor. Many years later Mary remembered all of the details — even the questions the teacher asked her. But especially she recalled the lunch hour.[4]

Abby and Martha wanted to show off their pretty little sister. They sat Mary on a table and asked her that question put so many times to children: "What do you want to do when you grow up?"

The youngsters crowded around curiously to hear her reply. The answer must have been in Mary's mind for some time. It came quickly, and it was so unusual that the pupils laughed. Most of the girls wanted to be mothers or teachers, while nearly all of the boys expected to be farmers. Never before had these country children heard of anyone — especially a girl — with an ambition like this.

"When I grow up," said Mary earnestly, "I want to write a book!"

5 *"Of my mother I cannot speak as I would, for memory recalls qualities to which the pen can never do justice."*
. . . Retrospection and Introspection
MARY BAKER EDDY

There are few people who have never been the object of faultfinding. Mary's mother may have been one of these few. Much good was said of her, but there is no hint of any criticism. She seems to have been especially loved by all who knew her, and Mary wrote of her years later as a "sainted mother in all the walks of life."

Where Mark was unyielding as iron, Abigail was persuasive and often able to smooth differences of opinion that arose between father and children. She reminded them: "Your father intends to do right and he loves you." [1] She had a gift for knowing the hearts of others, and her insight dissolved the pride and injured feelings that would have prolonged a disagreement.

Like all women of her time, Abigail Ambrose Baker held a secondary position in her home, her community, and her church. She could not join in her husband's conviction of a fearsome Deity majestically sentencing people to heaven or hell before they were born. However, at the same time she could not escape the feeling that it might be sinful not to believe as Mark did.

With few exceptions, women had no recognized rights. They could hold no office in the church or in town affairs. It was to be another century before women were given full voting rights. As a Massachusetts minister told the women of his congregation: "Politics, philosophy, mathematics, or metaphysics are not your province." Women, he said, must recognize "that consciousness of inferiority which for the sake of *order*, the all-wise Author of Nature manifestly intended for them." [2]

But pioneer women had shared danger and hardship with their men on an equal footing, and women like Hannah Lovewell Baker were not passive, submissive creatures. During the years that Abigail was raising her family, a half-dozen children were born in New England and New York who were to spearhead the revolt of American women for freedom. There were Elizabeth Cady Stanton, Susan B. Anthony, Harriet Beecher Stowe, Julia Ward Howe, and Lucy Stone. There was Clara Barton, founder of the American Red Cross, born the same year as Mary Baker. Some of these women were also to be prominent in the American struggle to free the Negro slaves.

Abigail could not enter into the government of her day, but her influence was felt nevertheless. She "governed her own house," as Mary once put it. Her children, her husband, and her neighbors respected her, not just for her kind, loving manner but for her capable handling of a large family and household. Management of a farm household in the early 1800's was no easy task.[3] Almost all spinning and weaving were still done at home, since textile factories were just beginning to be built in New England. There was little leisure as it is known today. Abigail might walk as many as fifteen miles a day in her work at the big wool wheel, which required three short, quick steps for each arm's length of wool fiber.

Mary's mother was twenty-three when she married Mark Baker. It was an average age for marriage; early marriages in this day were an exception.[4]

Abigail Ambrose was blond and blue-eyed, short and plump. She was a year older than Mark. The Ambroses lived on the east side of the Merrimack, and in his courting days, Mark used a canoe or the hand-poled ferry to cross the river.[5] He and his family attended church at the Ambrose Meeting House, which was just across the road from the Ambrose home, and it may have been at church services that he first met Abigail.

Abigail's father, Nathaniel Ambrose, was listed in the family genealogy as a farmer and hotel proprietor, but he was best known in Pembroke for his unswerving support of the Ambrose Meeting House and the Congregational Society. The meeting house had been named for him, and the story is told that he contributed so much time and money to its construction that he was eventually ruined financially.[6]

Mr. Ambrose was a deacon of the church, appointed to assist the minister. One of his duties was the "lining of the hymns." After he read a line or two aloud, the congregation would sing and so proceed through all the verses to the end of the hymn. There was at one time a small choir, accompanied by a bass viol — until a dissenter to this last innovation greased the strings![7]

Because both Abigail and Mark Baker were deeply devout, their religion played a strong role in the upbringing of their children. In addition to the daily prayers, Bible reading, and regular church attendance, Abigail impressed upon her children her own sense of a loving God.

She was especially close to Mary, who shared and responded to her mother's pure trust in God. Abigail read the Bible frequently to the little girl, and the two talked together about the stories of Jesus' healings. Mary felt a special joy in her mother's promise, "God is able to raise you up from sickness." Later, in her own reading of the Bible, she pondered Jesus' words, "And these signs shall follow them that believe; . . . they shall lay hands on the sick, and they shall recover." She felt a power in the statement she could not then fully understand.

"We need the supports of prayer," her mother explained, and Mary prayed often. She longed to be so close to God that she could understand all she read in the Bible. When she learned that Daniel prayed three times a day, she decided to do the same. She wrote her prayers in the style of the Psalms, writing and rewriting, trying to put the words into some form that would sound like the Bible. To pray seven times a day would be even better than three, she assumed. So for some time she kept count of these earnest daily petitions with a chalk mark on the woodshed wall.

No painting or photograph of Abigail Baker has been found. But her youngest daughter Mary treasured all her life the picture of her mother, with the golden hair and clear blue eyes, singing to her at bedtime:

How can I sleep while angels sing,
And hover o'er my bed;
And clap their wings in joy to Him
Who is their glorious Head.[8]

Abigail taught her children the common lessons of courtesy, neatness, and consideration for others. She soon learned that with Mary it was necessary to touch on some of these lessons more lightly. Her youngest child was by nature so neat that she was apt to cry over a wrinkle in her dress.

Lessons in thrift were a necessity on the farm. Abigail taught them by means of short maxims or proverbs, such as, "Waste not, want not." Years later Mary recalled her mother's concern for a single kernel of corn.[9] One evening the family was gathered around the fire, and the children were shelling corn for the chickens. As Mary shelled an ear, one kernel dropped to the floor. She pushed it toward the fire with her foot.

"Mary," her mother said, "get down and pick up that corn."

"Oh, Mother! It is only one grain," Mary answered.

"Never mind," said her mother, "it will help to make a meal for a chick!"

"Count that day lost whose setting sun finds no good done" was another of the maxims Mrs. Baker taught her children. Still another was the proverb from the Bible, "It is more blessed to give than to receive."

But Mary, who was so sensitive, sometimes took these maxims too literally. When she had just started school, she gave away her mittens, her cap, and later her coat, to children who were not dressed warmly enough for a bitter winter day. After she had given away her coat, which had meant long hours of spinning, weaving, and sewing, Abigail finally cautioned her, "You must not give away your clothes. Mother does not have time to make others."

The children of the Daniel White family, who lived near the Bakers on the Concord Turnpike, had lost their father. He had passed away about the time Mary started school, and his widow was hard pressed to take care of the family. The Bakers did all they could to help. Mark was not a skilled shoemaker and did not enjoy the task of repairing his own family's shoes, but he sat down to his cobbler's bench and made shoes for the widow White's children.[10] It may have been to these children that Mary gave her warm clothing.

Abigail taught her children to love one another, and they showed great affection toward each other as they were growing up. Family letters later mentioned daily prayers for each other. There were small family squabbles, of course. Occasionally the boys would get into a fight and end up refusing to talk with each other. This would upset Mary, who would take upon herself the role of peacemaker, running back and forth carrying messages between the brothers:

"George, you love Sam, don't you?" she would prompt.

George would agree reluctantly, and she would push her point: "You don't want to quarrel, do you?"

With a "no" from this brother, she would then rush off to confront Sam solemnly: "You love your brother George, don't you?"

"Yes, Mary, I do."

"Then you don't want to hold any ill will, do you?"

"I certainly don't."

"Then," she would declare triumphantly, "why don't you tell him so?" And, of course, by this time the quarrel was over.[11]

Mary's mother was well known for her readiness to help when others were in trouble. Many came to her for comfort, and by her own example she gave real meaning to her sayings.

Another of the old maxims was the familiar "Honesty is the best policy." Mary recalled for many years the time she innocently brought home a pitch pine knot from the neighbor's woods.[12] The knots were prized by the children because of the blaze they made when thrown on the fire. Her mother asked her where she had found it.

"In Mr. Gault's woods," Mary replied.

"Did you ask him for it?" her mother questioned. Mary admitted that she had not.

Her mother was stern. "Carry it right back again, Mary. It is stealing for you to do that, and God forbids you to steal."

Mary pleaded, "Must I carry it back now? I am so tired."

"Would you have God and mother thinking until tomorrow that you had broken His commandment?" was her mother's decisive answer.

6 *"My father possessed a strong intellect and an iron will."*
. . . Retrospection and Introspection
MARY BAKER EDDY

Mary once said that her father held his family in tighter harness than any she had ever known. Mark Baker was lean and erect and hard-working. He drove a hard bargain, his neighbors said, and he exacted the close obedience and respect of his children. It was his way of assuring a sound upbringing, although sometimes it seemed to the children that he was unreasonably stubborn in demanding that they bend to his will. Sternness and unquestioning obedience were the foundation stones of his sense of religion, and for him there was no separation between his religion and daily living.

Mark became clerk of the Congregational Church in Bow the year after Mary was born.[1] As soon as Mary was old enough, she drove with the family in the wagon to the Congregational services held in the Meeting House on White Rock Hill, near Bow Center. It was the custom to purchase a family pew, and Grandfather Joseph Baker had done so some years before.[2] Each family sat on benches enclosed by a low wooden partition. It was understood that one did not sit in someone else's place without an invitation.

The Meeting House looked very much like a large house or barn.[3] In fact, the instructions given by the Bow townspeople for its construction in 1792 read: ". . . build as large a house as that of Mr. Colby of Pembroke."

It was considered a handsome building, well-proportioned, built as sturdily as the best barns and houses of its time. Some of these structures still stand a century and a half later, square and firm as the day they were raised. The timbers were hand-hewn and massive, joined with large wooden dowels or pegs.

The interior of the Meeting House was plain but spacious. Opposite the front entrance was the raised pulpit. There were pews on the main floor and in the side balconies. First-floor windows and rows of high windows placed almost at the roofline above the balconies gave abundant light. As Mary sat with the family in worship, the great timbers supporting the high roof carried thoughts heavenward as well as any vaulted cathedral.

There was no stove in the Meeting House. Such pampering of congregations did not come into vogue until some time later. When stoves were finally installed, it was often over the violent protest of some sturdy old church member raised in the tradition of the foot warmer!

The foot warmer was a small tin box, pierced with holes, encased in a wooden frame and carried by a bail handle — much like a bucket. A small tin pan fitted into this box. Before leaving home, churchgoers filled the pan with glowing coals from the fire. The warmer was then carried into church for the ladies and children to use as a foot stove. Men were not supposed to need such niceties.

When Mark Baker became clerk of the church, the record book took on a precise, crisp tone. The first thing written in the book in his firm hand was the Confessions of Faith Recorded. One paragraph stated clearly his own creed regarding his children: "You believe that it is the duty of heads of families to train up the children under their care for GOD, by all good precepts and examples and by praying with and for them night and morning."

He did pray with his children night and morning.[4] And each morning when the family assembled on benches, Mark took the great family Bible from its special stand and read a chapter aloud.

Grandmother and Abigail Baker had no part in the services at home or at meeting, except as listeners. Women were expected to keep silent.

While all kneeled and closed their eyes, Mr. Baker prayed. Sometimes the prayer would turn into a sermon — and a long one. Mark Baker was a fine speaker, and he liked to talk. The words would flow on and on and on. Appropriate passages from the Scriptures would pour out as he continued with fervent zeal. No matter how threatening a storm might be, no matter how many tons of hay might be waiting in the field, nothing could stop him. These "sermons" were especially hard on the youngest Baker, who found keeping still for so long a difficult task. The rest of the family silently endured them.

But one day as her father talked on, Mary found it simply impossible to kneel any longer. Suddenly, in a flash of inspiration, she noticed the fat pincushion that was kept on a nearby table. Stuck into it were the long pins her mother used to fasten her shawls. No one saw her reach up, take one of the pins, then quietly crawl along the floor until she was right behind her father as he kneeled in lengthy petition. With a quick and well-aimed thrust, she accomplished what no one else had been able to do. The sermon came suddenly to an end! In the excitement that followed, Mary made her escape.[5]

Mark had ample proof in many ways that this child was independent and quick-witted. He was sometimes asked to settle quarrels among his neighbors. Though he himself was known to be at times hard to deal with, he had the reputation of being an intelligent and fair-minded man. Two neighbors arrived at the farm one day to ask Mark to help settle their differences. Mary sat listening, unnoticed in the corner of the room. Words flew back and forth. Then the argument became heated as one man began shouting. All at once she stepped in front of him.

"Mr. Bartlett," she said, "why do you articulate so vociferously?" The big words from the little girl broke the tension. Everyone laughed, and no one could be angry after that.

Big words came naturally to the child. She listened carefully, and she spent much time reading. She enjoyed trying to read the newspaper to her father even though she could not always pronounce the larger words. Several newspapers published in Concord brought the news of the world to Bow: A gentleman in France had made a rapid ascension in a balloon, and it was hoped he would touch mother earth again; western lands were for sale; there was an Indian war in the West; a young ladies' literary school was being established in Concord; there was a woolen factory to let; American grass bonnets and buffalo skins were for sale. "All news from abroad," the paper assured its subscribers, "came by latest ships."

If Mr. Baker was not reading, he was working at his desk. There were twelve small drawers on the top, each carefully numbered. Like most of his neighbors, he kept a close record of his finances in a journal-account book. Actually, very little money was exchanged. The accounts involved mainly barter and services, and there would be a settling when Mark and a fellow townsman compared books. At the end of the account would appear the notation: "This day settled and found even," or, if it were not found even, the note would be, "This day settled and made even." Mark would sometimes lend his oxen to Andrew Gault and balance this against his use of the Gault cider mill or oxen or some other service. Each item of business would be entered in the account book.

The entry for one typical November day read: "To a day of a hand [Mark referred here to a helper] and four oxen 3.00." The month before, Andrew Gault had helped the Bakers by "two days work . . . 1.34" and had also made them "twenty-one barrels of cider at his mill for 2.10." But Mark had given a "stick of oak timbers . . . 3.00" and "a day and a half framing . . . 1.00." The two had also traded heifers, and Mark Baker had come out "1.00 to boot."

Mark's wagon figured prominently in his account book. His neighbors paid him for trips made at their request to distant Newburyport or nearby Concord.

Some of the Bow farmers had only oxcarts. The Baker wagon must have been a good one, probably what was known as a pleasure wagon, with a wooden spring seat in front and room for placing a bench in back for the children. But the girls in the family did not enjoy riding in it. The fashionable conveyance of the day was a chaise, a two-wheeled carriage with a convertible top. Mark's daughters had not been able to talk him into the purchase of one of these more elegant vehicles, the sports car of its day.

On the girls' side, it should be stated that their father was a rather prominent man in Bow and might have been expected to drive a chaise, as did Esquire Brown and Esquire Rogers. Mark, too, was sometimes listed in the town records as Esquire, which indicated that he was held in respect. He had conducted town meetings, was often a member of the committee that settled the town's business each year, and was several times elected a selectman. But he would not buy a chaise! [6]

Mark was also a member of the New Hampshire militia, which had been formed in the days of the Revolutionary War. He was a sergeant major, fourth in command of his regiment, and required to possess the proper equipment, including a flintlock on the barrel of which was stamped a star and the head of an eagle. This gun, along with canteen, knapsack, powder horn, cartridge box, and bayonet scabbard, were later treasured by George Baker and passed on to his own son.[7]

It may have been in the militia that Mark first met General Benjamin Pierce, pioneer settler of Hillsborough. Their two families were related through a cousin. Though Hillsborough lay west of Bow and Concord a distance of about thirty miles, Mark Baker and General Pierce became good friends.[8]

General Pierce had fought in most of the important battles of the Revolutionary War. He was a familiar figure in the area, still wearing the old-fashioned tricornered hat, short breeches buckled at the knee, and high boots. He commanded the state militia at one time, and when

"If Mr. Baker was not reading, he was working at his desk."
Mark Baker's desk and personal possessions, including a sand shaker used for drying (blotting) the ink.
Baker Room, Longyear Foundation

Mary started school, he was governor of New Hampshire. Mark Baker sometimes visited with him in Concord. The General may have brought his son Franklin with him on visits to the Baker home. The young man was serving his first term in the state legislature when his father was governor.

Many years later, Franklin Pierce became the fourteenth President of the United States. In only a few years, he was to become an important influence in the life of Mary's brother Albert.

7 *"Many peculiar circumstances and events connected with my childhood throng the chambers of memory."*
...Retrospection and Introspection
MARY BAKER EDDY

Mark Baker worried about his youngest daughter. She was clearly different from her brothers and sisters. She seemed more sensitive and was apt to become concerned about things which some children scarcely noticed.

The cramped quarters and confusion of the one-room district school may have been difficult for Mary. A report of the School Committee for the town of Bow noted:

It is one of the greatest faults of our schoolhouses that they are *too small.* In many of them, there is no fair opportunity for necessary locomotion. Besides, the seats and benches are too narrow and contracted — sometimes *too high,* sometimes *too low,* while the scholars are huddled together, in the most uncomfortable ways imaginable.[1]

Maintaining discipline, too, was sometimes a problem in the early schools. Order was kept by means of "whippings" with the branch of a sapling or by boxing an unruly pupil's ears. The older farm boys in the room were often as strong as the teacher, and they were not always obedient and eager to learn. There were times when the master of a winter school might find himself tossed out the door into a snowbank.

In some towns, physical strength was considered nearly as important a qualification as a teacher's education. Rumor had it that at the schoolhouse where Albert Baker planned to teach a schoolmaster had to pass a test of strength in order to get the job. A very large cobblestone was said to be kept behind the schoolhouse. The new man was expected to be able to lift it easily and hurl it a certain number of yards to prove he was up to the demands of handling a classroom.[2]

For most young people schooling was a luxury snatched between winter storms, hard work, and family circumstances. The two sessions of the school year were short, sometimes only ten weeks each and with no regular schedule of terms from year to year. Teachers came and went, often staying for only a single term before moving on. The pupils' attendance was erratic, depending on the needs at home and their own health. There was much illness and much talk of it in diaries and letters.

Mary's attendance at the district school followed the usual uneven pattern, and it was sometimes interrupted by illness. But Mary took her lessons very seriously. She would bring her books home and put them under her pillow at night in order to study early in the morning.

Although Mary was considered more delicate than her brothers and sisters, she was high-spirited and lively. She did not hesitate to stand for what she felt was right, no matter what others might think.

Once there was a girl in the schoolroom who was ignored by the other youngsters. No one would play with her or speak to her. Mary invited the girl to sit next to her and extended her friendship. Finally the other children included the girl in their games and discussions, and years later she told how much Mary's kindness had meant to her.

One summer, when Mary was about eight, an older girl in the school delighted in teasing the other children. The teacher's whippings seemed to have no effect on her, and even the boys were afraid to stand up to her. She took special delight in tormenting the smaller children and made everyone so unhappy that Mary resolved to tolerate it no longer.

One morning the older girl picked up a cucumber on the way to school, scooped out the inside, and filled it with muddy water taken from the roadside. Arriving at school before the teacher, she came into the room holding the cucumber high in the air.

"Now," she cried to the younger children who had run to the far end of the room, "every one of you must take a drink from the cucumber."

The older girl was bigger than Mary, but the youngest Baker planted herself in front of the frightened youngsters.

"You shall not touch one of them. I will not permit it," Mary said.

The bully laughed, and shouted, "Out of the way, or I'll knock you over."

"No," said Mary, folding her arms, "you will not lay a finger on me nor harm one of them."

A look of amazement came over the older girl's face. "You are a brave little rascal," she said. And she threw her arms around Mary and kissed her.

It was not the last of the teasing; but Mary persisted in coming to the rescue of the smaller children until the girl gave up. The teacher observed that there had been a great change for the better.[3]

Mary enjoyed being outdoors. She climbed the stone walls and wandered through the woods and meadows. There was much to watch along the course of the pasture brook. Frogs sat sunning themselves on the rocks, tadpoles wriggled along the sandy bottom, and bright-winged dragonflies swooped low over quiet pools.

Mary and her sisters picked wild strawberries, blueberries, and blackberries in summer. In the fall, they gathered hickory nuts and sweet chestnuts to be roasted over the fire.

Mark liked to tease his youngest daughter, knowing how generous she was. He would say sadly as the children came home with their baskets full of nuts, "Now, who pities father?" He was never disappointed. Mary would immediately give him her entire basket.

Like most country children, Mary learned to be a good judge of horses. She once spoke of the joy of jumping on her favorite horse and galloping across the meadows, her hair flying behind her as house and barns were left far in the distance.[4]

Mary was encouraged to play out-of-doors because the family doctor felt that she thought too much and that her brain was too active for her body. He advised that she be kept away from school as much as possible and not be given too much medicine.

Her father took Mary out of school for a while, but taking away her books was not so easy. Wherever he hid them, she found them. To this day the story is told in Bow of how in the midst of playing with other children she would slip away and would later be found sitting on her favorite ledge reading a book.

It was impossible to keep Mary from thinking. She was often stirred by the heated conversations she overheard between her father and his guests. Her father's strong voice could be heard plainly by the child as she lay in her trundle bed in an adjoining room. One night Mary stayed awake listening to her cousin Aaron arguing with her father.

Aaron had been reading books on Universalism, a new religious doctrine which held that all men's souls would eventually be saved. Mark Baker believed staunchly that after death a man's soul went straight to heaven or to hell and stayed there forever. Mark felt it was his duty to save his nephew's soul from this dangerous new concept, especially since Aaron had lost his father some years before and so had not had the advantage of "proper" guidance in religious matters. As the two men went back and forth vehemently over the whole ground, Mary listened eagerly to every word.

On another evening her father discussed a Bible text for three hours with a friend, and again Mary was far too keenly aroused to sleep. When the discussion ended she went over and over the arguments and then prayed over the problem far into the night. The child, like her mother, went often to God in prayer. She longed to be close to Him, to know and to obey His will.

During the year that she was eight, Mary had an unusual experience.[5] One day she thought she heard her mother calling her. She answered, but her mother said she had not spoken.

"But Mother, who did call me?" Mary asked. "I heard someone call 'Mary,' three times."

This happened a number of times, and after a while Mary did not bother to answer nor to ask her mother whether she had called. One day, however, Mary's cousin Mehitable Huntoon came to visit. Mehitable was fifteen years older than Mary. She was sitting with her when the voice came again, and she looked at Mary, expecting her to answer. Finally she spoke sharply, saying, "Mary, your mother is calling you."

Mary went to find her mother; but as had happened before, her mother said she had not called. Then Mary explained that her cousin had also heard the voice. Abigail Baker spoke with Mehitable in an adjoining room. The door was ajar, and Mary listened anxiously as her mother questioned the cousin closely to be very sure that she too had heard Mary's name called. Mehitable insisted that she had.

That night, when she tucked Mary into bed, Abigail turned to the Bible and read the story of Samuel to her youngest daughter:

Now Samuel did not yet know the Lord, neither was the word of the
Lord yet revealed unto him. . . . And Eli perceived that the Lord had
called the child. (I Sam. 3.)

She told Mary that if the voice came to her again she was to answer as Samuel had done: "Speak, Lord; for thy servant heareth."

Later the voice came again, but Mary was afraid and did not answer. Afterward she cried, and prayed that she would be forgiven, promising that next time she would do as her mother had told her. When the call came once more, she was obedient and answered, "Speak, Lord; for thy servant heareth." Never again was the call repeated. Mary had given her answer.

8

"Among the treasured reminiscences of my much respected parents, brothers, and sisters, is the memory of my second brother, Albert Baker, who was, next to my mother, the very dearest of my kindred."
... Retrospection and Introspection
MARY BAKER EDDY

The Baker children were beginning their preparations for the winter school term. Like their friends, they had to make most of their school supplies. Copybooks were made by folding long sheets of paper and sewing them into covers of plain brown paper. Pens were fashioned from carefully sharpened quills, and brown ink was made from the bark of the swamp maple. "Plummets," or pencils, were made by melting lead and letting it harden in a shallow groove or a convenient crack between the floorboards.

In the midst of all this preparation, there was special excitement because brother Albert was to be the new schoolmaster. Albert had planned on one more term of teaching before going to college, and the opening had come at School #3 in Bow.[1]

It was 1830. Abby was fourteen, Martha was eleven, and Mary was eight. George was seventeen and now helping Mark with the farm. Samuel, the eldest, was now away in Boston.

It would have been contrary to Albert's nature to show favoritism in his classroom, but it was probably a great deal of fun for the whole family to talk over the day's events at supper and when they gathered around the fireplace in the evenings. As the term went on, Albert was impressed with Mary's ability to grasp the ideas he was discussing with the older children. He had known that his little sister had an unusual memory. At home she was a prompter for the entire family when anything needed remembering, and now he could see that she actually remembered nearly everything she read.

She struggled with the intricate hooks and trammels of the elaborate penmanship taught in those days. Her spelling was by no means ideal. But her vocabulary was far in advance of the other pupils' because of her constant reading.

An important phase of schooling in those days was the practice of public speaking. Everyone was expected to take his turn speaking a piece before the class. It was a time when great speeches were reported frequently in the newspapers. Statesmen rolled out long oratorical arguments like heavy cannons. Then their political opponents replied with their own speech-making artillery. In school, poems or parts of famous speeches were memorized and given with as much force and freshness as a student could muster. One of Mary's textbooks, earlier her brother Sam's, was *The Columbian Orator, Containing a Variety of Original and Selected Pieces Together With Rules Calculated to Improve Youth and Others in the Ornamental and Useful Art of Eloquence.* Edward Everett Hale, the noted New England author and preacher, born the year after Mary, once commented: "I owe to the public school and to this now-despised exercise of declamations that ease before an audience which I share with most New Englanders."

In New England town meetings no man was afraid to stand on his own two feet and voice his opinions clearly and at length in front of the assembled townspeople. He had already spoken before most of his neighbors many times as a schoolboy.

Albert Baker gave excellent training in this speaking of pieces. He was already an able speaker himself, with a magnificent voice. In only a few years it was to be said of him: "In manner he was always forcible, often eloquent, and at times his lips seemed touched with a coal from the very altar of truth." [2]

The school term came to an end all too soon for the Baker girls. In the spring, Albert left for Dartmouth College in western New Hampshire. With Albert away at college, life on the farm settled back into its usual pattern. At town meeting, Mr. Baker was elected a selectman, and Uncle Philip Baker was made a constable. Andrew Gault, their next-door neighbor, moderated the meeting. And, it is noted in the *History of Bow,* a musical trio was formed, Uncle Philip "on the bass drum, Jeremiah Morgan on Snare drum, and Amos Morgan on Fife." [3]

Mary felt particularly lonesome because Abby, too, was planning to go away. Determined to have more education, Abby would attend Pembroke Academy and board with the Burnhams, as Albert had done. [4] Sister Martha, also, was beginning to have interests outside the home circle. She sometimes stayed overnight with friends, and at eleven felt much more grown up than Mary.

When word was out that a circus was coming to town, George saw an opportunity to cheer Mary up. Imaginations had already been touched off like skyrockets by circus posters on barns and storefronts. Lions and tigers and jaguars and camels! Acrobats who had performed before royalty in foreign capitals! "The evening's Amusement will commence with military evolutions by SIX RIDERS . . . slack rope . . . tumbling . . . clowns," the posters promised. There was to be horsemanship and tightrope dancing by acrobats with baskets on their feet!

It was just as wonderful as imagined. The huge canvas tent hid a shimmering, unbelievable world. One of the clown's jokes was remembered long afterward by George and Mary. [5] According to the story recalled by Mary, there was a baboon among the circus animals. Said one of the clowns to the audience, "That baboon looks like Daniel Webster" (the New Hampshire senator).

Someone in the audience shouted back, "Look at me. I am Daniel Webster."

"The school term came to an end all too soon. . . ."
Original schoolhouse at Governor Dummer Academy,
Newbury, Massachusetts

"Well," said the clown with a flourish, "in that case, I do not know to whom I should apologize."

George Baker was becoming known in the Bow area as a talkative, exuberant fellow who had a way with the girls. He wrote long sentimental verses to his girl friends. Albert worried about him, and felt he was likely to get into trouble unless he learned to hold his tongue and control his pen. He once wrote to George:

Will you allow me to mention to you what I think a radical defect
in your character? It is want of prudence — prudence in your friend-
ships and enmities both. When you have an attachment, you confide
too much, and when you have a dislike, you are too unreserved in
discovering it . . . you take a man for a friend before you have tried
him . . . just count back how many clever fellows you have had for
confidents and see where they all are.[6]

Although Albert was widely liked, he was careful in the selection of his close friends. He had found two good friends who were to be a special help to him. Benjamin Pierce, the old governor, now retired to his home in Hillsborough, had taken a liking to Albert and felt he was a promising young man. And Franklin Pierce, his son, found much in common with Albert.[7] At this time he was conducting a law practice from the town of Hillsborough when he was not in Concord as a legislator.

During vacations from Dartmouth, Albert continued his active interest in Mary's education. He saw that she was working as diligently with her Lindley Murray *Grammar* as with the catechism which she had to repeat each Sunday.[8] The *Grammar* was divided into four parts: orthography, etymology, syntax, and prosody — that is, spelling, word derivation, sentence structure, and the meter and rhyme of verse.

The writing of verse was far more popular then than it is today. Friends included their own verses in letters to each other, and newspapers and magazines printed quantities of long, flowery poems. It was customary to express one's feelings in stilted, sentimental verses, all measured out correctly according to the rules of prosody.

Mary had the book-length poem called *Night Thoughts on Life, Death, and Immortality,* by Edward Young, and she noted in the margin the parts that Albert had read to her aloud.[9] Also among her books were the Lindley Murray *Readers,* some four hundred and twenty-five pages of fine print which included selections from well-known authors of the eighteenth century such as Addison, Pope, and Goldsmith.

It was a lifelong habit of Mary's to make notes in the margins of her own books and to underline passages which seemed to her important. In the *Readers* she had marked four articles on slavery and the unhappiness of the Negroes. Lines on national and patriotic matters were marked, and passages from the book of Proverbs were marked and numbered. Mary had drawn a line beside the observation:

To begin a story or narration, when you are not perfect in it, and cannot go through with it, but are forced, possibly to say in the middle of it, I have forgotten the rest, is very unpleasant and bungling. One must be extremely exact, clear, and perspicuous, in everything one says.

For a young person living in the country there was much in these books to catch the eye regarding the manners of worldly society. Mary had penciled the lines: "Awkwardness can proceed but from two causes; either from not having kept good company, or from not having attended to it."

While the youngest member of the family was bending all her energy to growing up, the eldest, Samuel, was starting a new life. On March 20, 1832, Samuel married Eliza Ann Glover, from Concord. Eliza's brother, George Washington Glover, known as Wash, was learning the building trade with Samuel in Boston. At the wedding, ten-year-old Mary met this handsome young man for the first time. In the midst of the festivities Wash swung Mary up on his knee and embarrassed her by asking her age and telling her that he would be back in five years to make her his wife.[10] Still involved in a little girl's world of family and friends, she ran and hid, little realizing that one day he would indeed come back to do exactly that.

Albert had noticed that it was natural for Mary to express herself in verse. At the age of twelve she was attempting serious poems modeled on the popular style of those she read in magazines and newspapers. One of her verses was entitled "On the Death of an Aged Friend." Another, called "Resolutions for the Morning," began:

I'll rise in the morn and drink in the dew
From flowers that bloom in the vale —
So mildly dispensing their charms ever new,
Over hillocks, and flowery dale.
I'll gaze on the orb in yon eastern sky,
For loftier thoughts 'twill invite!
His beams can enlighten the spiritual eye,
And inspire my pen as I write.[11]

Lines were scratched out, then several more of similar sentiment written in the same style. Some verses seemed thoughtful for a twelve-year-old poet.

Albert may have shared his Greek and Latin grammars with his sister on his visits home from college. He apparently gave her elementary lessons in these languages and in the Hebrew which he himself was studying between terms.[12] Mary loved to talk with him. He later mentioned in a letter to her the "discursive talking" or reasoning which she enjoyed so much.[13]

On his visits with his friends the Pierces, in Hillsborough, he undoubtedly shared anecdotes about this unusual little sister. To those who visit Hillsborough today, the story is sometimes told of a meeting Mary Baker is supposed to have had with Franklin Pierce. The future President of the United States is said to have advised her: "Learn all you can, Mary, and some day the State of New Hampshire will be proud of you."

9

"From my very childhood I was impelled, by a hunger and thirst after divine things, — a desire for something higher and better than matter, and apart from it, — to seek diligently for the knowledge of God as the one great and ever-present relief from human woe."

... Retrospection and Introspection
MARY BAKER EDDY

There was to be a new Methodist church in Bow called the Bow Bog Meeting House. Meetings of the society were held in the Bog schoolhouse while the church was under construction. It was to be a simple white building with green shutters and a squared-off steeple. The Andrew Gaults were members of the Methodist society, and the Bog road was not far from the Baker home. Thus it was probably natural for the Baker family to attend Methodist services occasionally. Baptists and Methodists along with the Congregationalists had made up the Union Church of Bow, and Mary once recalled that she was taught by both Baptist and Methodist ministers.

A Baptist church was being constructed at about the same time the Bow Bog Methodist Church was being built. It stood gracefully atop a knoll at Bow Center, another traditional little white church with cupola and weathervane.[1]

When the Congregational Society, always a small group, dissolved in 1829, the Bakers sometimes attended Congregational services in Pembroke and Concord. Mark and Abigail of course had strong ties in Pembroke, where Abigail's brother David and her father, Deacon Ambrose, were active. Mark's name appeared on the records of the church as early as 1811, when he joined the Parish Committee with David Ambrose. He was also a member of the Pembroke Sabbath School Society.[2] Mary and her brothers and sisters undoubtedly went to many of these Pembroke Sunday School sessions.

Mary received Sunday School instruction from several pastors. Although Mark could be vigorous in his arguments on church doctrine, he got on well with ministers of other denominations so long as they held essentially the same orthodox beliefs. The Reverend Mr. Boswell of the Baptist Church in Bow, the Methodist Elder "Father" Orlando Hinds, and the Reverend Abraham Burnham of the Congregational Church in Pembroke, all taught Mary at various times.[3] Mr. Hinds was a circuit minister, traveling by horseback to his church work in different towns. He was held in great respect and affection throughout the countryside.

Abraham Burnham at one time counted six towns, including Bow, as his parish. He shepherded his church for forty-two years. A fellow minister once characterized him as one who had "bold vigorous thoughts. . . . His hearers had their attention constantly directed to the Scriptures. . . . In moral courage, he was rarely equalled. He was also kind and warm." [4]

Many years later, in referring to these ministers, Mary wrote that the reason she loved Christians of the old sort was that she could not help loving them. "Full of charity and good works, busy about their Master's business, they had no time or desire to defame their fellow-men," she observed. "God seemed to shield the whole world in their hearts, and they were willing to renounce all for Him." [5]

Mark Baker's friend, the Reverend Mr. Burnham, was of this sort. His face showed the same strength of character as Mark's. The two men enjoyed many lengthy discussions, and Mark sometimes accompanied the pastor on his visits to backsliders in the parish. One can well imagine the success of these two in convincing such people of the grave error of their ways!

Pastor Burnham was a firm believer in Sabbath Schools for children and had championed one early in his own ministry before they became generally accepted.[6] As a friend of the Baker family and also a pioneer in the Sunday School work then just beginning, he contributed much to Mary's religious education.

In the first year of the 1830's, Mary's Grandfather Ambrose and his family moved away from Pembroke. This may have influenced the Bakers' decision to join the Congregational Church in Concord in April, 1831. Abigail Baker's uncle and two cousins were already members there. Cousin Nathaniel Ambrose, named after his grandfather, was a respected deacon of the church.

The move to the Old North Church, as it was called, was an exciting one for the Baker family. The church was the largest in the state. The youthful minister, the Reverend Dr. Nathaniel Bouton, was stirring strong enthusiasm among young people and drawing crowds, averaging seven hundred worshipers, to hear his eloquent Sabbath sermons.[7]

At the time the Bakers joined, Nathaniel Bouton was just beginning his ministry. Traveling by horseback, he managed to call on each family in the large parish at least once a year. He visited the sick regularly, and delivered lectures and conducted Bible classes throughout the area. He seems to have understood young people and was highly successful in encouraging them to join his Bible classes.

A Sabbath School session, comprised of young and old alike — nearly the entire congregation — was held after the second service on Sunday. The children were taught the Westminster Catechism, verses of Scripture, and hymns. When the Bakers became members, there were fourteen Sunday Schools in the parish, each taught in a different place. Since the Bakers had to travel several miles into Concord and stay during the day, Mary attended the Sabbath School which was held at the church.

The Old North Church in Concord was an imposing structure, two stories high, with a tall delicate spire, and seating twelve hundred people. Mary often recalled the great elm in the churchyard, where the family ate a picnic lunch and visited with relatives and friends between the morning and afternoon services.[8] On a summer day, the yard was grassy and studded with buttercups and daisies.

As the Bakers approached in the pleasure wagon, they could hear the sexton ringing the heavy bell in the steeple — setting it occasionally on its head, and taking care that the rope did not pull him off his feet. When the Reverend Dr. Bouton, his wife and children appeared at the door, the sexton would stop his jigs and flourishes and toll the bell with sharp, staccato notes. If the Bakers were still on the road, they knew they must hurry to take their places inside.

The pulpit was elevated and reached only by a narrow flight of stairs. It loomed up, as one member put it, "like Mount Sinai, in awful majesty," high above the congregation. Over the pulpit and the minister's head a large sounding board, suspended at an angle from a single iron rod attached to the ceiling, was designed to throw the minister's voice out, so that those in the farthest pews could hear. Children in the audience sometimes whiled away lengthy sermons by wondering, with a shiver of expectation, if the sounding board would someday fall down!

As the Bakers settled in their pew, the bell ceased to toll and there was a short prayer. The benches, Mary discovered, were as hard as those in the Bow Meeting House. But there was one innovation she found most interesting. The wooden seats were hinged, so that when she stood up with the family at the beginning of prayer, the seat did likewise. And, when she sat down at the close of the prayer, as did the rest of the congregation, all the seats went down with one emphatic bang in response to the minister's amen.

Sitting near the Bakers was one of Mary's contemporaries, the Reverend Dr. Bouton's son John, who half a century later, wrote a colorful description of the service.' The introductory prayer, he recalled, was "rapt and serious, as of one who communes with God — clear, but well pitched and heard by everybody."

Next came a hymn. The leader of a small chorus blew the proper
note on his pitch pipe, sang out, "do, re, me, sing!" and his little band

responded. Several years later, the Concord church had a large choir, supported with musical instruments — usually a violin, flute, clarinet, bass viol, and double bass. The minister's son remembered that the man at the bass viol made "wild dabs at the strings." The organ was a still later addition.

After the Scriptural reading, came the *event* — the sermon:

The church deacon clears his throat and straightens himself in his seat as an example of alert attention. There is a rustle all over the house as of skirts being adjusted . . . a little clatter of footstools being comfortably fixed.
When all is quiet, and not until then, the minister rises to preach. The sermon is doctrinal, for sure, after the fashion of the period. . . . The people wanted no other kind. . . . The higher criticism is yet unknown. The pastor and his flock are not plagued with problems which are soon to shake the foundations of belief. . . . As currants on a bun, or raisins in a pudding . . . [the sermon] is stocked with Bible quotations. . . . And so text is heaped upon text and proof upon proof.

Thus, the son, who also became a minister, remembered his father and his father's church with reverence and love fifty years later — as did Mary Baker.

If the pastor and his flock were not plagued with problems, one small member of the congregation was beginning to struggle with a problem very serious indeed to her and to her father, who was steeped in the same doctrines as the good minister. For Mary, religious matters did not seem distant in the future or in the past. They concerned her now, and she felt she must understand and properly resolve them. For Mary, a religious truth was just as substantial, and must be as straight, as one of the stone-wall boundaries in her father's fields.

However, on a warm summer day, looking forward to a picnic lunch under the grand old elm, Mary Baker was probably as interested in visiting with her many friends as they were with her. The hour and a half between the morning and afternoon sermons was put to good use, with the steady exchange of family news and gossip, and a basket lunch which included doughnuts, cookies, and turnovers.

Then back it was to the afternoon service. When members had come a number of miles to church, nothing less than another substantial sermon would pay them for their trouble, although the afternoon sermon was possibly a shade less doctrinal than the morning's.

10

"In confidence of faith, I could say in David's words, 'I will go in the strength of the Lord God: I will make mention of Thy righteousness, even of Thine only. O God, Thou hast taught me from my youth: and hitherto have I declared Thy wondrous works.' (Psalms lxxi. 16, 17.)"
. . . Retrospection and Introspection
MARY BAKER EDDY

In spite of many similarities, Mary and her brother Albert differed in certain important ways. Albert had a sharp mind, and enjoyed probing, analyzing, and disputing. For her age, Mary was equally keen in her reasoning. Unlike Albert, however, she felt something deeply compelling in her young religious life, and as much as she loved and admired her brother, she was quite willing to pursue her own path.

When she was older, Albert once wrote her, "Though I may differ with you in all these matters of belief, it is far from my wish to discountenance religion." [1] He went on to assure her that he did not deny religion a place in his "affections." But it was clear that for Albert religion could be put off to a secondary place; for Mary, it must be primary.

While Mary was growing up, she undoubtedly went with her parents to church revival meetings held in Pembroke and Concord. Such meetings, then popular throughout New England, aroused a church and a community to a pitch of intense concern for religious matters.

Their purpose was to "save" those who had not yet professed their faith.[2] Revivals were sometimes called protracted meetings because they lasted far beyond the limits of a single church service. With the assistance of traveling evangelists and neighboring ministers a series of sermons and prayer meetings would be arranged. Then nearly every other activity stopped in town or on the farm. Many who lived out of town stayed overnight with friends and relatives, since the meetings sometimes continued far into the night, and went on day after day, with time out only for sleeping and eating.

Those who were already "saved from perdition" would try to awaken others to concern for their spiritual welfare. Wives would speak earnestly to husbands. Men would ask their neighbors whether they had not yet become "anxious" about their condition or made plans to "come forward" at the next meeting. Young people, too, were included in the revivals. Children sometimes repented in front of the meeting and "obtained a comfortable hope," even though young persons were not usually given church membership.[3] The Concord church, like many others of this period, did not generally accept children as members.

Between 1814 and 1835, the Congregational Church in Pembroke held eight revivals, each one, according to the church history, "exceeding, in interest and power, its predecessor, till the number of the church had increased from 50 to 240."

The members of the First Congregational Church in Concord voted in March, 1834, when Mary was twelve years old, to hold a protracted meeting. It was to commence on Monday, the twenty-eighth of April. The church record book states that in the meantime members were "earnestly to implore the blessing of God on themselves and on the extraordinary means of grace that may be used for the conversion of sinners and the promotion of the redeemer's kingdom." On April 10, the congregation voted to observe a day of fasting and prayer preparatory to the protracted meeting. A committee was appointed to "make all

necessary preparations, lighting the house, also seating arrangements."
Five neighboring ministers were to assist the Reverend Mr. Bouton at
the revival.

As Mary heard of plans for the meeting, which was to be the most
important church event in a number of years, she perhaps felt she had
reached a point where she should profess her faith. Jesus' childhood
experience at the age of twelve was a compelling example, and children
of this age were often encouraged to ponder it.[4]

Mary knew that to come forward and have her profession accepted
by the church members she must agree to certain doctrines, including
the view that everlasting punishment was administered in the afterlife
to those who had not been saved. The "Manual for the Use of Members
of the First Congregational Church" stated most emphatically in the
Articles of Faith:

You believe that there is one true God, the Father, the Son and the
Holy Ghost. . . . That man has fallen from the state in which he was
originally created, and is by nature entirely destitute of holiness. . . .
In the everlasting blessedness of the righteous, and the endless
punishment of all the finally impenitent. . . . Thus you believe?

None of her brothers and sisters had made any profession of
religion, and Mary could not believe that because of this they would go
to hell, while she would go to heaven if she accepted the faith.

Mary was not alone in questioning the doctrine of predestination
or unconditional election. The winds of freedom were blowing through
New England, stirring the minds of many. A number of books had been
published which took issue with the doctrine. In 1820, the year before
Mary was born, Nicholas Baylies, in the adjoining state of Vermont, had
written *An Essay Concerning the Free Agency of Man*. The book
circulated in Bow, and Albert may well have mentioned it to Mary.

New England was thinking for itself. Within the next decade a group
of its thinkers known as Transcendentalists — Ralph Waldo Emerson,

Henry David Thoreau, Bronson Alcott, and Margaret Fuller — would emphasize the goodness of God, the goodness of man, and limitless possibilities for the human race. Also a sturdy faith in the self-reliant individual was growing. The pioneer nation which had accomplished so much in such a short time showed a tendency to refuse to give in to anything as inevitable — even the will of the Almighty.

Of course, for Mark Baker and many other New Englanders at this time such an idea was heresy. When he discovered that his youngest daughter was apparently rejecting the belief in everlasting punishment, he was gravely displeased. Not only was he concerned that her soul would be lost, but his pride was wounded. As a man of some importance in the church, he found it most disturbing to have his daughter voice her disbelief in a basic church doctrine.

As the meeting drew closer, Mark came into direct conflict with Mary.[5] He argued with her long and vehemently, as he had with Aaron Baker. His thundering assertions of "right" and "wrong" upset the whole household. Mary was by nature and upbringing an obedient child. But she could not and would not alter her conviction. Both father and daughter had the Baker determination. Both undoubtedly felt they were being obedient to God's will.

Mary's mother had encouraged her trust in the love of God. Would He be a God of love if He had predestined some to be saved and some to be condemned? Fearlessly she told her father that she could not accept this doctrine of the church. Mark stormed, and Mary became ill. Forgetting everything then, except his love and his fear for his child, Mark went for the doctor. The diagnosis indicated a severe fever. Abigail stayed close by and bathed Mary's forehead with cool water. She urged her daughter to rest in God's love. As in the past, she was sure that Mary could go to God in prayer and seek His guidance.

As Mary prayed, she found her happiness quietly returning. Soon the fever was gone, and she was well again. All that day she and her mother felt they were borne up by an inner joy. The physician was greatly surprised. And the arguments for predestination no longer frightened Mary or seemed impressive.

The protracted meeting commenced Monday night, April 28, and lasted for seven days.[6] The Bakers doubtless stayed in town with relatives for the duration of the revival. There was a prayer meeting at dawn on Tuesday, followed by morning, afternoon, and evening sermons. Wednesday's pattern was the same but with an additional prayer meeting and an evening of "singing, prayer, and exhortation."

On Thursday, a sunrise service, held at the Town Hall, was followed by exhortation and a noon prayer meeting. In the afternoon the Reverend Abraham Burnham delivered a sermon, the second in his series of four. The Bakers' friend then addressed the children and youth, certainly Mary Baker among them. One church member noted in her diary: "Inquirers met at the schoolhouse. Many went and desired to be prayed for." Six more sermons polished off the week!

The revival sermons were sometimes referred to as the cannonading, and the talking or arguing with the repentant or anxious person afterwards as hand-to-hand combat. At the end of a sermon, the sinner might answer the call to come forward to the anxious seat. This was usually a pew located at the front of the church, and there the minister or an assistant would talk earnestly for some time with those who had come forward. He might describe in colorful terms the tortures awaiting those who were lost, praying with the little group and encouraging them to accept the chance for salvation while it was still held out to them.

When Mary's turn came to go forward, she was ready for the minister's doleful questions. She was willing to trust God, but she could not believe in the decree of unconditional election. The minister was startled. Mark sat stiffly, his face set and scowling. Abigail and the children were alert, straining to hear. Mary's trust in God was evident, but she would not admit to the doctrinal point.

The minister shifted his ground. A little more gently, perhaps, he asked when Mary had experienced a "change of heart," a typical revival phrase. Mary was by now in tears. She said that she could not give a precise time. The clergyman tried again. She had been truly regenerated, he insisted. Now she must describe how she felt when the new light dawned within. Mary paused, and then it came to her that she could answer in the words of the Psalms she knew so well. She replied that she could only repeat what the Psalmist had declared: "Search me, O God, and know my heart: try me, and know my thoughts: and see if there be any wicked way in me, and lead me in the way everlasting."

This was spoken with such pure conviction that some of the church members wept. Because children were not usually accepted as members, Mary did not join the church at this time, but she had made her profession of faith, however unorthodox.[7] It was not to be the last time that her most deeply felt convictions held firm in the face of great pressures to conform.

11

"During my childhood my parents removed to Tilton [Sanbornton], eighteen miles from Concord, and there the family remained until the names of both father and mother were inscribed on the stone memorials in the Park Cemetery of that beautiful village."
. . . Retrospection and Introspection
MARY BAKER EDDY

For the Baker family, the years at Bow were coming to a close. Early in the year of 1835, when Mary was thirteen, Grandmother Baker passed away. Mark no longer felt an obligation to keep up the old homestead. As Albert put it, he was "talking of a thousand things," among them, farms in nearby Sanbornton.

In the summer of this year, George decided to leave home. He was twenty-two years old and desired to strike out on his own. However, he may have selected this particular time because of a certain young lady

Do not I hate them, O LORD, that hate thee? and am not I grieved with those that rise up against thee?

22 I hate them with perfect hatred: I count them mine enemies.

23 Search me, O God, and know my heart: try me, and know my thoughts:

24 And see if there be any wicked way in me, and lead me in the way everlasting.

PSALM CXL.

David prayeth God to deliver him.

To the chief Musician, A Psalm of David.

DELIVER me, O LORD, from the evil man: preserve me from the violent man:

own

10

let the

pits.

11

blish

viole

"She . . . could only repeat what the Psalmist had declared. . . ."
Bible page

and some poetic letters. George's letters had fallen into the hands of a rival for the young lady's heart, creating a small-town tempest in a teapot.[1] And worst of all, the young lady had chosen the rival.

It had thus seemed expedient to George that he leave immediately for Connecticut. He made the trip with a Mr. Cutchins, a family friend who worked in the Wethersfield state prison.[2] The warden was Amos Pilsbury, son of Moses Pilsbury, warden of the New Hampshire State Prison in Concord.[3] Through these acquaintances of the Bakers, George was able to obtain a position as foreman of the prison shops.

Mary wrote George one of her first letters. Until two years earlier, in 1833, mailing letters had been costly and irksome for the residents of Bow because there was no post office. But when Mr. Clough was made postmaster, and his general store the post office, the sending of letters became easier, though it was still expensive.

The cost of sending a single sheet was so high that it was customary for an obliging person to carry the letters his friends and neighbors wished to send along in the direction he was traveling. In fact, Mary justified the "second letter I ever wrote" by explaining that Mr. Cutchins, George's Connecticut friend, would carry the letter to George and thus save "that expense which any intelligence that I could communicate would but ill repay." [4]

It was the practice for all the members of a family to add their bits to a letter in order to save postage. Up to this time Mary's letter writing had usually been confined to adding a sentence or two in family letters to Albert.

Her first letter to George shows the affection the Baker children felt for each other. Mary writes that she has

lerned from experience to prize more perhaps than ever I did *before* that is *Dear brother* . . . the lively interest you ever manifested in my welfare but now when I sit down to my *lonely* meal I have no brother Sullivan to encourage me as formerly.

Her spelling and punctuation still left much to be desired. But it was an unusual letter in the early 1800's that did not depend heavily on the individual's own best guess for the spelling of less common words. George Washington and many another prominent man of that day would not have lasted long in a grammar school spelling "bee."

Mary chatted on briskly and gaily. The sentences flowed into one another just as they would in a face-to-face conversation; and she underlined continually for emphasis.

George was apparently concerned over his father's displeasure at his hasty departure, but Mary assured him, with tongue in cheek, that their father had said he felt the change was necessary for George's health. Always ready to tease, she volunteered the information, already too well known to George, that "in this Town *far kened* and *noted* is *your name* and we are in daily expectation of receiving some of your *poetical* effusions a love ditty or something of the kind."

She closed with a typical touch of Baker humor, evidently referring to a gift and message sent with Mr. Cutchins: "Thanks for the present you sent me by Mr. C. although I did not receive the tooth pick I shall take the will for the deed and think much of them for coming from you."

Albert had now graduated from Dartmouth with honors, and was living in Hillsborough. He was studying for the law and assisting Franklin Pierce in the latter's legal practice, but he had been visiting at home in Bow when George left for Connecticut. He had stayed on a week to help his father finish the hoeing, one of the chores George had apparently left undone on his sudden departure.

Albert sent to George by letter some of the advice he frequently dispensed to his younger brother and sisters. He wrote that he was

very much pleased to find that you had made such improvement in your hand-writing. With a little care, pruning some of your letters of a few cragged flourishes, . . . you will soon write quite a decent hand.

But more than all, it gives me pleasure to perceive that you have concluded to look upon the world like a *man in his senses.* It would puzzle the devil, at least me, to guess or even conceive, what it is, that has benumbed your wits. . . . If we would make anything of the game we must play it ourselves, and play it dexterously, not even trusting another to look into our hand. . . . Treat every man civilly, courteously, honestly, but take care of yourself, or none else will do it. . . . I stayed a week after you left and in the course of that time *we* finished hoeing. He [father] got his pet over immediately, and was better humoured, and enjoyed himself more in that week than in any apparently, this six months. . . . School begins in a fortnight.

Albert's law studies had to be financed, even though the Pierces were generous in their help to him. He had accepted the position as principal of Hillsborough Academy which was located near the Pierce home.[5] Abby, who was teaching a district school in Hillsborough, planned to attend Albert's school at the end of her term. She spoke of remaining at the academy "until I graduate . . . or get some mark of distinction."

Both brother and sister appear to have been living with the Pierces, and there Abby had her first taste of a more elegant way of living.[6] Although the elderly Pierces were simple pioneer folk at heart, Franklin Pierce was a polished young gentleman. The Pierce home was furnished in the latest style; the parlor had magnificent scenic wallpaper imported from France, and there was a ballroom on the second floor. There was a formal garden with an artificial pond and a latticework summerhouse.[7]

Abby attached a postscript to one of Albert's letters to George, written at the end of July, in which she mentioned that their father was selling the farm in Bow. Now a young lady, she had very definite ideas of her own about the social graces and social standing, and the old farm no longer seemed fine enough. She wrote to George: "Well, I am glad of that if he does not get a worse one. But . . . he cannot very well get a worse one."

Mary did not share Abby's feelings about the old homestead. She always thought of it with affection. Later she was to write of it as "the dear old farm and this with all its cares and toil." The Bow years were, she said, a part of "the golden days of my childhood."

New England was moving into the era of the industrial revolution. Factories were gradually replacing farms. Wherever a waterfall along a river could furnish power for a woolen or cotton mill, a mill town sprang up. These were poor counterfeits of the old New England town. Instead of the village green surrounded by the meeting house, gracious homes, and broad meadows, there were apt to be strings of similar houses huddled together bleakly near the doors of the dominating mill.

Mark Baker and his brother Philip were excited over the possibilities of one of the mill towns. According to the Reverend Dr. Bouton's *History of Concord,* from about the beginning of the year 1835 there was a:

remarkable spirit of *speculation,* amounting almost to a mania. Visionary schemes were projected, airy hopes raised, and extrava- gant sums paid for land, with the expectation of amassing thereby a large fortune.

This particular bubble burst in 1837, but before this, Mark Baker had made plans to buy property in Sanbornton, eighteen miles north of Concord. The village at the southern end of the town was known as Sanbornton Bridge, later called Tilton. At the Bridge the Winnepesaukee River tumbled through the town, affording ideal waterpower. It was said that property was rising in value and would continue to rise rapidly. As soon as he could find a suitable place, Mark would move his family.

Mary had turned fourteen that July of 1835. After Mark had finished the haying, he wrote George with satisfaction that he sold the crop for a good price and then purchased a supply in Sanbornton. In this way he avoided hauling the hay to a new home.

The old farm was sold to Josiah Rogers, a prosperous neighbor who was buying up a number of properties in the area. Rogers had purchased Uncle Philip's land several months earlier. Philip had moved to Sanbornton before Mark, but became ill shortly afterwards and passed away in 1837.

With autumn and the preparations for leaving the farm, Mary must have felt a penetrating sadness. The "golden days" at Bow were almost over. She would often walk down to the river where it flowed past the Baker property. She liked most of all to go at sunset, when the water was streaked with the varied hues of the setting sun.[8]

As Mary sat on the bank of the Merrimack, the sun dipped behind the Bow hills. In the quiet of the evening, ripples lapped against the shore. A boatman's horn echoed across the water startling a flock of wild pigeons so that they whirled up into the evening sky. There was only the occasional leap and splash of a salmon and the chirping of birds settling in their nests.

12

"My childhood's home I remember as one with the open hand."
. . . Retrospection and Introspection
MARY BAKER EDDY

Mark and Abigail had decided on a farm in Sanbornton about a mile from town.[1] However, Abigail's heart was not in the move. She became ill just before they left the old home and did not recover completely for some time. Mary, too, was sick at the time the decision was made to leave. But Mark proceeded with his plans, hauling two loads of the family belongings to Sanbornton in November. Albert came for a visit in December, probably for a last look at the Bow homestead.

Mark missed his youngest son's help. In September, he advised George to stay where he was if he could make $15 a month "for there is much said in this place about you." However, by November, talk about George had subsided and his father urged him to return home, although admonishing him, "I do not want any more answers in parables, say yes or no."

Albert had this advice to give his brother:

One thing is certain, if you have saved your money, you have done better the past year than to have stayed at home, for father has done all that both of you would have done, and you have your wages left. . . . Father works like a slave, but he dont know how to manage. . . . You must go home, and stay at home, and mind your business and keep at work — *have no more intrigues and write no more letters.*

George's decision was to remain in Connecticut. He was keeping a journal, was reading Shakespeare, and composing poetry. He filled page after page of his journal, pouring out his loneliness in the midst of the dreary prison surroundings where he worked. In one of his verses he wrote:

A father's hand, support to yield a Mother's tender, heartfelt sigh, A brother's smile, inspiring hope, a sister's tear of sympathy A heart that beats as none can beat but those that love in constancy All are withheld, and I alone may know the bitterness it yields.

His writing was usually emotional; sometimes his pent-up feelings seemed to explode on the page. Like the others in the family, Albert did not take the younger brother's literary efforts seriously, but he did see in them the need for strong self-discipline.

The older brother wrote in one of his letters that he was thinking of going west, perhaps to Mississippi or Illinois. (That was as far as the Far West extended for most Americans in 1836.) Albert also mentioned that he had been ill. His health did not improve, but he continued to drive himself — sometimes, it would seem, beyond the point of common sense.

"She would often walk down to the river where it flowed past the Baker property. . . ."
New Hampshire countryside

Parting with their friends in Bow was a sad experience for the Baker girls. Mary had a special affection for Andrew Gault. One of the poems she wrote at this time was for him. The poem was flowery but expressed her sincere feelings, and Andrew valued it so highly that he carried it with him when he went to the Midwest three years later.[2]

The Saturday before the Bakers moved, in January of 1836, their young Bow friends gave the girls a farewell party. Several young men escorted them to the affair at neighbor Esquire Parker's home. "It was," Martha reported to George, "one of the finest parties you ever saw . . . not so great as it was good."

The family planned to make the final move the following Monday. Abby had returned from Hillsborough and was living at home. She and Martha had flatly refused to be seen riding to their new home in the wagon, and Martha reported to George that "we like to had a dreadful fight about it."

Mrs. Baker, always tactful, had arranged for two young men who owned chaises to drive the older girls to their new home. The fight seems to have been over who was to go with "the gentleman from New York," and who was to go with the childhood companion, Daniel Gault. Abby rode with Daniel! On Tuesday, Mary left the farm with her father and mother.

The house in Sanbornton was somewhat like the old one in Bow, except that the roof was not the long, slanting saltbox type. The house rested on the crest of a gentle slope, surrounded by fields and woods. Mark hoped to paint the house and build a new shed. He had, in fact, proposed to George a cash interest in the farm which would help finance this project.

The main road from Sanbornton Square to Sanbornton Bridge curved southward from the Square over several hills, and by the Bakers' door. It continued on to the Bridge past Sanbornton Academy and into town.

Despite its mills, the Bridge was a pretty village. It was to be some years before it took on the more somber look of a factory town. A broad main street bordered the river. On either side of the street were homes and stores, pleasant buildings usually white, with picket fences and gardens. At both ends of Main Street were small mills grouped around the waterfalls that furnished power.[3]

The arrival of the Baker family created quite a stir in the social life of the village. The girls brought with them a touch of the manners and fashion to which they had been exposed in Concord. Little differences in the newcomers' ways were quickly noted. On her first day of school, Mary Baker had the girls agog with her new hair style called the French twist. She made friends at once by showing the Sanbornton girls how to do their hair in this fashion. She also made at least one enemy who was to recall the incident years later with a sharp tongue and perhaps a degree of envy.

But the three Baker girls were attractive and quickly made acquaintances. "Oh, but there were fine-looking girls in Tilton [Sanbornton]!" one schoolboy remembered years later, " — and wasn't Mary Baker one of them?"[4] There was a bustle of social activity with many invitations extended and accepted, *except* to dances. Mark did not allow his daughters to dance. Martha did attend one ball "without leave" when their father was away. She confessed to George she "experienced friction in the joints as a result of the unaccustomed exertions!"

Seated at the old table in the midst of the confusion shortly after the move, Martha wrote George for all three sisters. She remarked that her mother was still not well, gave other bits and pieces of news, and concluded her letter, feeling sorry for herself:

There is one place we have not been to neither am like to, this is to the dancing school that is only one mile from us. Now just think Brother how provoking it must be to be situated within reach of so much enjoyment, but not allowed to extend a hand.

By April, sister Abby was able to report to George:

We go on finely here, almost as well as we could wish. The people
are very kind and hospitable, we find society very agreable and
refined.

At the end of six months, she had turned down a suitor and had caught
one of the most eligible bachelors in town! Of these first few months,
she wrote:

We have had cards and compliments in profusion, to attend dancing
schools, balls, and parties. Of the latter we have attended a number,
and were highly gratified with the proceedings. Balls and dancing
schools we have not frequented.

All was well with Abby, except for one thing:

If our buildings and furniture were a little more splendid, and we
had a chaise, I think we could appear to much better advantage; but
it is extremely mortifying, to my pride, to push off to meeting in a
waggon, here we are so far from meeting that we cannot walk and
we must ride in such an old vehicle, or stay at home; but here is one,
that will stay at home, rather than ride in such style.

And there was a postscript to George signed by Martha:

You know our situation here — you know our natural dispositions &
I want you to use your influence in removing one particular source
of embarrassment and chagrin; this is prominading the streets in a
waggon. I know Father can get a chaise if he will and if he does not
I will not go to meeting a time this summer & I shall tease him this
way about it. Should you write dont pray implicate us.

The letters passing back and forth so frequently now between
George and his sisters were sometimes carried by Mr. Cutchins. He
visited the Baker family again the first of May, and returned to
Connecticut with two letters for George, one each from Martha and
Mary. Martha wrote:

Father and Mother have just retired and left Mr. Cutchins and us
girls to amuse ourselves; so he and I are writing. Mary is reading
and Abbie sits and orders me what to say but I shall not regard her. . . .

Sullivan, they do act so bad it is impposible for me to write and I wish you could make them behave for they keep shaking the table and making me laugh all the time, and now they have brought on a bowl of apple-sauce and a plate of nuts and turnovers and a pitcher of sap beer [from the sugar maple tree, boiled down and flavored with spruce twigs]. Now do you wonder I cannot write.

Mr. Cutchins, who was to carry the letter, added his own postscript:

This is the most pleasant spot that fortune has had the kindness to place your friend C. . . . It does not flow with 'milk and honey' but maple sugar and molasses in abundance. Plenty of all the dainties of life and a multiplicity of fine girls.

Mary waited until the next morning to compose her letter, saying she preferred solitude. Although her letters were lively and humorous, she used a more literary style than did her sisters. First she modestly told George that she would not attempt the formalities of letter writing. Then she said:

I shall resign that office to Martha, for you know 'she holds the pen of a ready writer,' still I hope after I read the book you sent us, I shal becom some what more civilized in my presant state of ignorance. . . . We have some fine ladies up here, perhaps as fine as you ever saw, but none, I conclude, that will exceed the fair Maids of *Cont.* [Connecticut]. We have enquired of Mr. Cutchins how far you have crept into their good graces, but have not acertained, and now brother, what *wait* you for?

The youngest sister could not keep from adding a sly reference to the wagon:

You cannot imagin the disappointment I felt on receiveing your letter that you should not return . . . hopeing time still continues to glide smoothly as in former years, it continues to do so with us, only when we are obligeed to ride in a wagon and then it is rough.

Brother George, from the safe distance of Connecticut, tried to intercede for his sisters. He was caught in the crossfire for his efforts. His father replied tersely to him:

> With respect to the Schaise I do not feel able at present to purchase
> one and lay no claim to the bargain.

George's final report on the matter referred the girls to the Bible, and brought a wail from Abby:

> I do not understand when you speak of the chaise you refer us to the
> 28th of Job . . . but my will remains inflexible and I shall not attend
> meeting in a waggon this summer.

Abby took over the village school for the summer term and lived at the Bridge, going home once or twice a week. Fortunately for her, there were a number of young men all eager to give her a ride, and doubtless in a chaise.

As in Bow, Mother Baker welcomed visitors. The girls often had parties, and young people were always in and out of the Baker home. There was the usual pitcher of syrup, cool and clear for tasting at maple sugaring time, and there were turnovers and doughnuts, and apple sauce and sap "beer" — always something good to eat for one visitor or a dozen.

Mary turned fifteen in July, Martha was seventeen, and Abigail twenty. Mary attended the district school at Tin Corner near her home that summer.[5] She received instruction from Sarah Bodwell, the capable and well-educated daughter of the Reverend Abraham Bodwell, the Congregational minister at the Square. Mr. Bodwell was a Harvard graduate and moving spirit of the Woodman-Sanbornton Academy. Sarah later became preceptress or principal of the "female department" of the Academy.

Because Congregational services for the Bridge were held across the river in Northfield, the Bakers sometimes went to church at Sanbornton Square. Martha reported to George that "we had a great sing at Mr. Bodwell's church."

It must have been a happy summer for Mary. She was making fast friends with her neighbor Priscilla Clement. The two were to correspond for many years. Another good friend was Augusta Holmes, with whom Mary carried on a lively correspondence.[6] The Holmes family and the Bakers met at town meeting, and the girls of both families became devoted friends. Nathaniel Holmes was owner of one of the large cotton mills located on the river. Augusta's brother had attended Dartmouth with Albert and was also a lawyer.

The Bakers had Albert home that summer for some weeks. He had become ill again and had decided to return home to try to regain his health. Samuel also came up from Boston for a visit.

Mary was of course overjoyed to have Albert back in the family circle, even under these circumstances. Topics that the brother and sister could merely touch upon in letters were now fully explored.

Albert, Martha, and Mary all came to know Sarah Bodwell that summer. Since Abby was teaching and boarding in town, Sarah may have boarded with the Bakers. The schoolhouse was nearby, and the Baker family often kept the schoolteachers. In Sarah's "memory book" a full page is inscribed by Martha, a terse remark is signed "Baker" by Albert, and another full page is written by Mary. The youngest Baker all her life placed a high value on lasting friendship. Her message, so lengthy that she had to squeeze in the last few, finely written lines, was devoted to that subject.[7]

Albert wrote at the end of August to George:

I have been at home now three weeks, and hope my health is some improved. . . . Mary has attended school all summer. . . . Martha commences going next week, when Abigail's school closes. Apropos of that Abigail, *they say* she is going to get *married*. . . . She may have told you of a ride to the White Hills with one Mr. Tilton. . . . Father is as happy as a *clam*. . . . He lives in the neighborhood of two Sanctuaries — a matter of the greatest moment — two Academies, a very pleasant village, society agreeable etc. etc. He has cut a grand crop of Hay though corn and grain are miserable. No matter he likes it and that is enough.

Mark Baker was indeed happy. He liked being close to town and its activities. And now his oldest daughter was to marry into one of the leading families.[8] Alexander Tilton, Abby's fiancé, twelve years her senior, held a partnership in a general store. He had successfully operated two others and a woolen mill, also in partnership with others. The marriage was set for the next summer. The first of the three Baker sisters was about to leave the family circle.

13

"My father was taught to believe that my brain was too large for my body and so kept me much out of school, but I gained book-knowledge with far less labor than is usually requisite."
... *Retrospection and Introspection*
MARY BAKER EDDY

The Baker home was situated between two schools, Sanbornton Academy to the south at the Bridge, and Woodman-Sanbornton Academy, several miles north at the Square. Sanbornton Academy was a plain, two-story wooden building. The classrooms were drafty, and there was not a single stove.[1] But it was nearer the Baker farm than the Woodman school, and both Mary and Martha hoped to attend. Sessions were held in the fall and occasionally in the spring.

Martha began classes in the fall of 1836. The family apparently had an agreement that one daughter would remain at home to help with chores while the other attended school.

Both Mark and Abigail Baker encouraged their daughters to continue school when it was possible. However, education was still regarded by most parents as a frill, desirable when convenient but given up at the whim of a student or the need for help at home. Usually the only men in a small town who had been to college were the ministers, doctors, and lawyers. In one hundred years of Sanbornton history following the Revolutionary War there were only twenty-two college graduates from the town.

A fine school committee in Sanbornton, made up of well-educated men, was struggling to better the system.[2] One member of the committee complained in a lengthy report on a typical district school that "no notice was given when school commenced or *if* it commenced," that "there was great irregularity in attendance," and also that "the scholars suffered very much from the cold."

Martha reported to George towards the beginning of the new year that she had started school but was forced to stop:

You know how little regard is had to the temperature of the school rooms and I soon found that the little exposures which I suffered were making secret depredations on the little health I had secured.

Mary wrote that she had been studying at home "every leisure moment all winter." Because of her natural curiosity and determination, her education was a continuous process whether in or out of school.

George also heard from Abby, who said that their father "has been remarkably prospered." He had cut a fine crop of hay that season, had hauled in the lumber to build his shed (George had evidently contributed some money to the project), and had "the finest woodpile in town."

In this second year at Sanbornton, Mark added a new friend, the Reverend Enoch Corser, to the group of intelligent, forceful men with whom he felt at home. The Reverend Mr. Corser, a graduate of Middlebury College, was to have an important influence on the education of Mark's youngest daughter.

Enoch Corser came to the Bridge in 1837 from nearby Loudon, where he had been minister of the Congregational Church for over twenty years.[3] He was about Mark's age, and like Mark possessed a somewhat unyielding disposition. A difference of opinion with his parishioners in Loudon had led to his decision to leave for Sanbornton Bridge. It was Sanbornton's gain, for the new minister brought a needed drive. Within a year, a new Congregational Church was built on Main Street.[4]

Mr. Corser was a scholar and a deep thinker. He was a heavy-set man, with a thick head of silvery hair and compassionate eyes that carried a humorous twinkle. A church member described him as

a man of powerful voice and tremendous muscle, which he often used on the desk and Bible in his moments of intense fervor. He used to marshall all his forces of invective against the wrong, and his attacks were nothing short of storm and siege.[5]

The new minister was also a master of extemporaneous speech. As he became filled with his subject, another church member recalled, he would rise by degrees "to admired eloquence and deep pathos; often fastening the attention in breathless silence." [6]

He had been a teacher for three years in Massachusetts, and on his arrival at the Bridge was immediately engaged as principal-teacher for Sanbornton Academy. At the same time, Mark Baker was elected with him to the board of the Academy as a trustee. Mark served in this position for eight years, was president of the board for two terms, and a member of the executive committee.[7] In the latter position, it was his duty to raise money for the Academy, probably the most difficult problem faced by these early high schools.

The Corsers and the Bakers became good friends, and before long Mr. Corser recognized Mary's intellectual capabilities. He had tutored his son Bartlett so thoroughly that the young man entered college already qualified in the required mathematics, Greek, and Latin. Now he began to tutor Mary.[8]

Mary may also have attended classes at the Academy. For the years that Enoch Corser conducted the school there are no attendance records available. The good minister had his hands full shepherding both the church and the Academy, and administrative paper work was kept to a minimum. Under his guidance, at least six weeks of instruction were usually given in September and October to twenty to thirty students.

Even though Mr. Corser was a staunch Calvinist, Mary found him a sympathetic and dynamic comrade. Despite the years between them, the two spent many hours discussing religious questions. They remained good friends even when they could not agree.

Mr. Corser considered Mary not only brilliant but marked for some special achievement. He once said to his son, who was one of those young men who called at the Baker home: "I never before had a pupil with such depth and independence of thought. She has some great future, mark that. She is an intellectual and spiritual genius." [9]

It is significant that Dr. Hildreth H. Smith, Mary's cousin and an educator of note, said years later of the girl, as he looked back, that Albert was considered "one of the ablest lawyers of New Hampshire; but Mary was deemed the most scholarly member of her family." [10]

However, Mary's concern for thinking through a problem by no means interfered with her spirited nature. A relative once referred to her as "gay, light-hearted and frolicsome." [11] The young men of the town were discovering that the youngest Baker sister was not only an attractive young lady, but also full of fun and one who added much to the life of a party. She was slim and graceful, with expressive hands and refined features — a delicate straight nose, firm mouth, and high forehead. Most striking and doubtless most devastating where the young men were concerned, were Mary's eyes. Their color was always a matter of controversy, for it seemed to depend on the light and the color of clothes she wore. From black to violet, to blue, to grey, the color might range. But no one ever questioned the beauty and expressiveness of those large deep-set eyes and dark lashes.

At a party Mary Baker was always surrounded by young people. She sang well, had a lively sense of fun, and a wit that quickly punctured the silly and pompous.

Albert wrote regarding one Sol Wilson who had fallen from Mary's good graces: "What is that poor devil doing? I hope you treat him as he deserves, with entire neglect." At about the same time, he sent her a letter which introduced a friend who was going to the Academy. He recommended him as a "sterling fellow, a little *enthusiastick* . . . a very close student, and is as much given to *discursive talking* as yourself, though he has not quite so much poetry at his command."

That Christmas Mary wrote to George about Albert's plans:

You have perhaps heard Esqr. Pierce is elected senator to congress. Albert remains at Boston and we believe considering the proposals Esqr. P. has formerly made to him that he will *now* relinquish the idea of going to the West.

Franklin Pierce had asked Albert to take over his law practice in Hillsborough and had also requested that he supervise the care of his aged mother and father at the family home.

Parties continued throughout the holidays. But that winter both Mary and her mother were not well. Nearly everyone in town was complaining of some disease, Mary told George. It was blamed on the severe weather. Mary applied herself diligently to her studies at home, evidently tutored by Mr. Corser. She planned to resume school the following summer. As spring arrived, she wrote George of her concern over Martha, who was now very ill: "I should think her in a confirmed consumption *if I would admit the idea,* but it may not be so, at least I hope not."

She did tell George that her spirits were "rather depressed today," but she managed nevertheless to give a gay description of a wedding she attended with a Mr. Bartlett: "He was groomsman and I bridsmaid: we had a fine time I assure you."

John Bartlett lived in the neighboring town of Hill, across the river from Sanbornton. He was Mary's age — sixteen — and was sometimes mentioned in her letters. John was a bright young man and wanted to be a lawyer.

George still spoke of returning home sometime, and Mary asked, "will not our brother make one in the number of our limitted circle ere long?"

Evidently he was giving Mary brotherly advice, perhaps passing on a little of all that Albert had given to him. Mary felt it necessary to explain apologetically:

I always write to [you] from the impuls of the moment, and to improve them as they fly would be adhering to the advice you gave me in your letter which was received very kindly.

She added that the writing master from the village was urging the Baker girls to attend his classes, but that "Martha is not able and I have not wherewith." The small amounts needed for schooling of any kind often presented a problem, and brother George loaned the girls money for this purpose several times.

There was one item in Mary's letter that probably came as a shock to George. She wrote:

Father has been speculating of late, although it is an allusion that in a letter might be considered rather abrupt, to tell you he has swaped your favourite horse with Mr. Rogers. And he thinks it a fine trade. . . . Abigail is prepareing for the celebration of her nuptials . . . then there will be another tie severed, she will be lost to us irrevocably, *that is certain,* although it may be her gain. . . . How changed in one short year! Dear brother . . . just take a retrospect view of home, see the remaning family placed round the blazing *ingle* [fireplace] scarcely able to form a semicircle from the loss of its number.

Several months before Abby's scheduled marriage in July, Mary became desperately ill. Martha wrote George that for a time she "gave no signs of recovery." However, shortly before the wedding Mary was improved enough to be carried out for a ride.[12]

Abby was married in July. Martha's health had been restored sufficiently so that she and Albert could be attendants at the wedding, but Mary was still not well enough to be a bridesmaid.

Samuel came up from Boston for the ceremony, and with him his brother-in-law Wash Glover, who was now in business in South Carolina. Mary must have again charmed Wash. The dashing bachelor, eleven years older than Mary, asked her to write him. But South Carolina was a long way off, and the correspondence was not to flower until much later.

Martha had a relapse after Abby's wedding and could not attend school as she had planned. All in all, Martha and Mary spent a good deal of the year confined to the house. They kept their spirits up, however, receiving visitors, writing letters, helping with the housework, and amusing each other for hours by playing their favorite game of Authors.

Albert had begun the practice of law in Hillsborough. He did so well that he wrote George in the fall:

My business has become worth . . . $1000 a year. . . . If my health continues, I shall not be quite so dependent as I have been. I have given up all idea of the West at present.

A thousand dollars was a large yearly income in those days, especially in a small town like Hillsborough.

Albert was active in public affairs. His speaking ability was outstanding, and he was asked to give many speeches. He was becoming known in political circles as a young man of great promise.

In his success, Albert did not forget his family. He wrote home regularly and continued to show a thoroughgoing interest in the welfare of his sisters and his younger brother. He complimented George in one of his letters, saying:

I received a letter from Martha yesterday. Her health is improving and so is Mary's. . . . Martha tells me she commenced going to school at your expense, but was obliged to abandon it. . . . One thing you deserve their warmest gratitude for your innumerable acts of kindness.

But he still felt it necessary to reprimand George. He was always the teacher, a reformer at heart. Referring again to George's volatile temper, he said, "I thought that you would cool down as you grew older but I believe it is the reverse."

George apparently took exception, and then Albert took the younger brother sharply to task:

One would think from the style of your letter that all the furies were at work within you . . . a friend chides, an enemy flatters. . . . See how long a time you can pass without suffering your feelings to be embroiled; and be sure that so long as *your* feelings are quiet, the feelings of those around you will be. Will you try?

George did try, and at this time he decided to heed the pleadings of Mary and Martha and his father. He returned home and entered the mill business in partnership with Abby's husband, Alexander Tilton. The latter had once operated a mill, George had experience in the prison shops, and Abby doubtless saw an opportunity for both husband and brother. George and Alexander purchased the site of what had been the oldest mill in Sanbornton and built a two-story woolen mill. One full set of carding machines provided the first step in the process of cleaning and sorting wool fibers.

The new venture was to make Alexander successful and Abby, in time, one of the town's wealthiest women. Mark Baker, too, prospered from the move. He was now able to sell wool to Tilton and Baker, and he received advice from his son-in-law on investing his money. Abby's husband built a fine house on a bluff overlooking the mill, and the Tilton home became a center of social activity.

Whether having his youngest son at home mellowed the father or whether Abby and George united in their efforts to bring more elegance to the Baker household is not known. But in this year of 1838 the town records do show that Mark Baker bought, not a chaise, but even more stylish — a carriage!

"... The elegance was temporary. In 1840 the carriage vanished from the records. ..."
Pleasure wagon, Old Sturbridge Village

True, the elegance was temporary. In 1840 the carriage vanished from the records and presumably the wagon returned. In the meantime the girls had their day. They rode in style to meeting, thus keeping up with Mrs. Tilton, as they often referred to their sister in the formal manner of the period. Abby herself in conversation and letters referred to her husband as Mr. Tilton.

In the summer of 1838 Mark and Abigail Baker withdrew their membership from the Concord church. Apparently they had kept their membership in Concord while they questioned whether to join Mr. Bodwell's church at the Square or the Congregational society that met across the river in Northfield.[13] With Enoch Corser's arrival and the construction of the Sanbornton-Northfield church on Main Street at the Bridge, Mark and Abigail made their decision to join.

The new church with its simple lines departed from tradition in only one respect: it was the only church for miles around that had a bell in the cupola. From its place in the graceful white steeple, the bell rang out every noon and every evening at nine o'clock.

Mary joined the Sanbornton church a month after her mother and father. It was a natural step, for her church experience followed closely that of her parents.[14]

Her friend Augusta, confused over church doctrine, possibly because of Mary's positive position regarding the doctrine of everlasting punishment, wanted to join with Mary. They discussed at length the "trials and temptations" involved, but finally Augusta could not bring herself to fully believe or disbelieve the articles of faith.[15]

Mary disagreed vigorously with Enoch Corser on the matter of unconditional election, and once again there was a struggle that made her ill. But she had found in her minister an understanding counselor. Recognizing her spirituality, he was willing to receive her into the church despite her disbelief in this particular doctrine.

With the yielding of his stern orthodoxy, Mary took the step with joy and a sense of peace.

When she stood up before the revival meeting in Concord at the age of twelve, she had, in effect, declared herself a child of the church. She had a "comfortable hope" and now it blossomed into church membership.

At age seventeen, Mary was one of the youngest persons received into active membership at the Bridge church. The church deacon who conducted the young woman's preparatory lecture was Elias Abbott, a saintly old gentleman who had held the position since the organization of the church in Northfield some sixteen years before. Mary Baker wrote gratefully many years later of the experience:

> I took my first feeble footsteps side by side with my revered parents. . . . Reverently I remember those solemn obligations which I so early assumed, and my daily prayers, then, and now, were and are to live a Christian life. . . . I recall with tenderness the smile of old Deacon Abbott at the close of preparatory lecture, and the pious prophecies and promises to pray for their church child.[16]

14 *"My favorite studies were natural philosophy, logic, and moral science."*

> . . . *Retrospection and Introspection*
> MARY BAKER EDDY

The Bakers plunged into church activities. At worship services and prayer meetings they faithfully occupied the square white pew numbered forty-five, a compartment approximately in the center of the auditorium, in line with the pulpit. Martha was a charter member of the Ladies' Circle, Mark was superintendent of the Sunday School, and George sang in the choir. A choirmaster taught the group, which sat in the singing gallery at the back of the auditorium. One church member recalled that the music was:

more pleasing to the congregation than the leader. To reinforce the time and tune, a trombone, violin, flute, clarinet, single bass and double-bass viol were added. Those were stirring times; and the little church rang like a music-box. . . . The audience used to rise and turn about twice every Sunday to witness the grand performance.[1]

Mary at this time was teaching the infant class in the Sunday School. At seventeen, she was a slender five feet six inches tall. Her dark chestnut ringlets set off a glowing complexion and deep sparkling eyes. One of her pupils recalled:

She always wore clothes we admired. We liked her gloves and fine cambric handkerchief. She was, as I have come to understand, exquisite, and we loved her particularly for her daintiness, her high bred manners, her way of smiling at us.[2]

As the girls in the district school had discovered, Mary had a certain instinct for looking fashionable under nearly all circumstances. When she attended church, she wore a graceful cloak over a silk gown, and a chic bonnet covered her curls.

After the services, Mary would return home each week to remember unhappily that the family's chore boy, Lyman Durgin, had missed Sunday School once again.[3] Lyman, who was eleven, had lost his mother some years before. His father had remarried, and Lyman did not get on well with his stepmother. Mark needed a chore boy, and Hazen Durgin, who lived near the Bakers, brought his son to the Baker farm. Mark liked the boy at once, and Abigail and Mary quickly took the lonely youngster to their hearts.

After a time, Mary discovered that Lyman did not attend Sunday School because he was so poor at reading. He seemed unable to memorize Bible verses as the other children did. Mary took the situation firmly in hand. She began to tutor Lyman, and through her patience and faith in him she was able to increase his confidence. First, she would read a Bible verse aloud, then close the book and rehearse the verse with him. When he was not faced with the unfamiliar-looking words, he discovered he could remember. Soon he was reciting in Sunday School.

Mary worked with Lyman for four years. Finally, he was so free from his early limitations that he left the Bakers' farm to serve an apprenticeship, and eventually became a master mechanic for a large railroad in the West. He always remembered Mary's kindness and kept with him the small Bible she had given him. Many times he was to tell his children of the young woman's painstaking care for "the awkward, ungainly boy that I was." He recalled that those four years were the happiest and most productive of his life, and said of Mary that he "had never seen anyone with such a glowing, radiant beauty."

During her tutoring of Lyman, Mary was pursuing her own education. Her former teacher in the district school, Sarah Bodwell, was now the principal of the female department at the Woodman-Sanbornton Academy in Sanbornton Square.[4] Miss Bodwell was teaching that summer, and Mary evidently decided to take advantage of her excellent instruction. Mr. Corser's school was not in session.

There were academies in many of the larger towns in New England, and it was not unusual for a young person to go to more than one academy. No transcripts or records of grades were required in that day, and students sometimes chose an academy simply because it was near relatives or in an interesting part of the country. Sometimes a certain teacher or special courses might attract pupils.

The high school, as it is known today, was developing at this time in New England and elsewhere, but education even in the elementary grades had yet to obtain the full support of the community.[5] Higher education was available only in towns where civic-minded groups took on the responsibility of sponsoring and financing an academy. It was an expensive undertaking, and ordinarily a nonprofit one. Some academies flourished, but many did not.

Since most students did not go beyond high school, the academy offered courses of study in subjects that were later found only in college. Much depended on the preceptor (or principal) and the instructors. If they were well-educated themselves, the courses would probably be at a high level.

The Woodman Academy was an excellent school. For several years the principal was Dyer H. Sanborn, the author of *The Normal School Grammar* and *Sanborn's Grammar*.[6] The latter was a popular textbook for many years and appeared in eight editions.

As preceptress of Woodman Academy, Sarah Bodwell was thorough and strict. She was considered an outstanding teacher. Her method of instruction required weekly essays from each pupil, but Mary, like many another student, occasionally waited until the last minute to begin her homework. She would sometimes arrive at school without the required essay, then have to dash it off at odd moments during the day. But the results were usually surprisingly successful. Sarah Bodwell was impressed with her ability and once said to her as she looked over her work, "Mary, some day you will be a distinguished author."

The Woodman Academy at the Square was a two-story building beside the Congregational Church and the Town Hall. The three white buildings in a row were all surmounted with graceful cupolas. In 1839 there were "33 Young Gentlemen and 23 Young Ladies" enrolled at the school.[7] In addition there were "3 Private Recitations." It is possible that Mary, who studied well on her own, sometimes took advantage of these private sessions.

Along with the usual courses at the academy, young ladies could avail themselves of instruction in needlework, drawing and painting, and in the pianoforte. Always, of course, there were prayer meetings and worship services. One academy advertised the choice of a "thorough English, mathematical, classical or ornamental education."

At that early period some young women dipped only their toes in the waters of education. But Mary Baker did not choose an ornamental course of study. Her favorite textbooks were Comstock's *Natural Philosophy* and *Chemistry,* Blair's *Rhetoric,* Whately's *Logic,* and Watt's *On the Mind and Moral Science.*

In the curriculum of the middle 1800's, the subject designated as natural philosophy included the general study of the natural sciences and astronomy. Mary's textbook discussed at length the discoveries of the English astronomer, Sir William Herschel. It surveyed "the causes of the earth's annual motion," the planets, the moon, and the earth, and such topics as air, sound, and optics, including refraction and the angle of vision. Gravity, the laws of motion, and the mechanical properties of fluids were also thoroughly examined.

Comstock's *Chemistry* — three hundred and forty-five finely printed pages, with numerous experiments to be performed by the student — was for its time a competent study of the subject. Twenty elements had been known to John Dalton, who had revived the study of atomic theory in 1803; about fifty of the more than one hundred elements known to us today were given by Comstock.

Blair's *Rhetoric* was one of the standard texts used in the schools of this period. The question and answer method was employed extensively, and Mary was later to make good use of this technique in her own writing.

Logic and moral science were among Mary's favorite subjects. Discussions with Albert had sparked her interest, and she was fascinated by the discipline of careful reasoning. Watt's *On the Mind* was an especially likable sort of book. The writer gave the impression of being a helpful friend rather than a pedantic, older person who considered himself superior. The author's strong faith that it was possible to rule one's own thought and make it do what one wished was supported by his heartfelt conviction that God would assist

"The Woodman Academy at the Square was a two-story building
beside the Congregational Church and the Town Hall."
Now the town library at Sanbornton, New Hampshire

in a practical way. He suggested some specific prayers for the young person to use before beginning his studies, and he counseled: "Offer up . . . your daily requests to God, the Father of lights, that he would bless all your attempts and labors in reading, study, and conversation."

The following passage in Watt's *On the Mind* may have caught Mary's eye:

The present age, by the blessing of God on the ingenuity and diligence of men, has brought to light, such truths in natural philosophy, and such discoveries in the heavens and earth, as seemed to be beyond the reach of man. But may not there be Sir Isaac Newtons in every science? Nor should a student in divinity imagine, that our age has arrived at a full understanding of everything which can be known by the scriptures.

Since public speaking and reading aloud were considered important skills, considerable emphasis was given at the academies to the use of the voice. *The Rhetorical Reader,* "consisting of instructions for regulating the voice," was a widely used textbook. It discussed articulation, inflection, strength and pitch of voice, timing, and audibility. Acquaintances of Mary remembered her voice as musical.

As a result of her schooling, her natural facility for expressing herself, and possibly Sarah Bodwell's encouragement, Mary began to think of herself as an author. Her first effort had been accepted by a local newspaper when she was sixteen. As time went on she contributed a number of poems, essays, and stories to several New Hampshire newspapers. Nearly always one column in a newspaper of this time was devoted to poems and other literary efforts by local contributors. Articles were sometimes reprinted from larger newspapers such as the *New York Evening Post* or magazines like the new *Godey's Lady's Book.* The magnetic telegraph had not yet come into its own, and one Concord paper boasted that European news was "only twelve days away." News often took the form of letters from those who were visiting various parts of the country.

One of Mary's poems was printed in the *Belknap Gazette,* a newspaper published in a neighboring town.[8] She seemed on her way to achieving the goal foreseen by Miss Bodwell: she would become a "distinguished author." But the path was to be far more difficult and to lead much higher than Mary Baker ever dreamed.

15 *"The trend of human life was too eventful to leave me undisturbed in the illusion that this so-called life could be a real and abiding rest."*
... *Retrospection and Introspection*
MARY BAKER EDDY

The year 1839 was an exciting one for the Bakers. Albert had been elected to the New Hampshire House of Representatives from Hillsborough. The House met the first of June, in Concord. The Bakers sometimes stayed with friends and relatives in Concord, and undoubtedly they went to the capitol to see Albert take his place at his first session of the legislature. During that session, he was to be on the Judiciary Standing Committee and chairman of the Select Committee on the Subject of Slavery.

Albert and many of his fellow members supported the right of the states to determine their own action regarding slavery. He opposed the agitation of the Abolitionists and he ended his committee's report with the prophetic statement:

That the slave must and will be emancipated at some future day cannot be doubted. But an event of such magnitude is not to be brought about in a moment. It will require years for its accomplishment; and he that would attempt it rashly, heeds little the consequences that must ensue.[1]

For the legislature, the purchase of land by the railroads inching up through the state was a difficult problem. There were thickets of ethical questions for every mile of progress. Albert championed the cause of the farmer. As his letters to George had indicated, he was a reformer.

His sympathy was with the underdog, and from the outset he proved he was someone to be reckoned with. His eloquent voice was heard loud and clear for the next several years as he challenged the railroads. He was called a Radical by the opposition; but he stood by the farmer who was being forced to sell his land to the railroad at the railroad's price. One of these farmers was his boyhood friend Daniel Gault, who had lost part of his property when the railroad cut through his land in Bow.[2]

It was in 1830 that Mary took one of her first long trips. She planned to visit friends in the suburbs of Boston, and set out in the stagecoach which left daily from the Bridge. It is likely that she rode in one of the famous Concord coaches made at the state capital.

The Concord coach was made of the finest wood and the toughest forged iron. Elegantly upholstered and gaily painted, it had seats for nine passengers inside, and six, plus the driver, outside.[3] There was rhythm in the roll and play of the wheels — but not enough to absorb the shocks of the rutted, stony roads. The driver cracked his whip, the team of matched horses responded in spirited fashion, the coach creaked, and was off. And Mary and her fellow passengers tossed and jounced on the red velvet seats.

The railroad had pushed as far as Nashua on the New Hampshire-Massachusetts border. There Mary may have changed to the cars of the Nashua and Lowell Railroad Corporation. This could well have been her first train ride, since the railroad had opened only four years before, in 1835. It was a dusty, long trip, and Mary must have been somewhat tired when she reached Boston. During her visit, she probably stopped to see Samuel, who lived in one of the three-story brick houses in Boston, in the heart of the city.

Mary put her thoughts about this trip into a poem. She was impressed with the gardens and the variety of trees she had seen, and she wrote a long, lighthearted description in verse.[4] Then, for the last lines of the poem, she took up the mournful tone that was so characteristic of the popular poetry of the day:

But clouds are a presage, — they darken my lay:
This life is a shadow, and hastens away.

Mary was always writing. When she was not composing poems or school compositions, or hopefully contributing to newspapers, she was writing letters to friends. Augusta Holmes, though she lived only on the other side of town, was one of Mary's correspondents.[5] The two girls were studying together, probably with Enoch Corser, and notes flew back and forth between them. George Baker or Lyman Durgin served as convenient couriers. George may have delivered some of the letters, packages, and schoolbooks which the girls exchanged, on his way to and from work, since Augusta's home overlooking her father's mill was not far upstream from the Tilton and Baker mill.

In one of her notes to Augusta, Mary remarked that she had found an essay. It "must be yours," she wrote, "will forward at the first opportunity." And in the same letter she asked:

Have you Surwalt's gramar? If so, would you do me the favour to loan it to me for a short time? I am told it is easier than Levizac's [French grammar] — at least if it is not I shall have the *horrors* worse than last evening — *after you left.*

She also sent her love to Abby, who lived not far from Augusta. Abby may have taken Augusta with her occasionally when she visited her parents. The older sister was a devoted daughter, and went out to the farm often. Mary sometimes returned with Abby and stayed in town at her home overnight.

In another note, Mary and Martha invited Augusta to a party. But in a long postscript Mary reminded her "to bring along with you that favourite book of mine, — I have not had an opportunity to send to Concord for one yet." Her thought was never far from books even when there was a party on her mind.

Milton, Shakespeare, Wordsworth, Scott, and Byron were all represented in her reading now. But the Bible was still the keystone, as it was to remain all her life. Evaluating its unique influence, she wrote in later years: "The Bible is the learned man's masterpiece, the ignorant man's dictionary, the wise man's directory." [6]

George Baker, at this time, was acting as constable for the town of Sanbornton and was also an active member of the twenty-ninth regiment of the militia, considered the best in New Hampshire. Eventually, he became a colonel on the governor's staff.

It was a grand day for the town each autumn when Muster Day was held in the large field behind Woodman Academy. Mary had been providing news of George's regiment to the *Belknap Gazette,* and she was on hand as local correspondent. [7] The boys in town had talked about nothing else for weeks in advance. Long before daylight of the holiday they started for the Academy. The parade was held in early morning, and they wanted to be present for every detail of the preparations.

Peddlers' and vendors' carts and gingerbread stands lined the parade ground. The Bakers and Lyman Durgin, the chore boy, were in the crowd as the companies of the regiment drew up in a dignified line opposite their respective headquarters' tents. The movements of the inspector-general and his aides seemed painfully slow. They scrutinized each knapsack down to the cartridge box, priming wire, and brush. The long silence was punctuated with the sounds of each musket and ramrod being shaken, each flintlock being snapped. The officers proceeded down the long line and disappeared from sight. The sounds grew fainter in the distance.

At last, the thin, high music of the fife and the roll of the drums could be heard at the far end of the field, and the grand march began. Later a brass band performed, led by cousin Amos Baker, Uncle Philip's son, who lived at the Square. Highlight and glorious conclusion of the day was the staging of a sham battle.

97

Except for such grand events, life seemed to be continuing much as always. George Baker and Alexander Tilton were doing well in their mill. Mark was selling wool to his son and able to make some investments with the increased income. Albert's career was showing promise of great success.

But Mary was not entirely happy. In spite of her close friendship with Augusta and the good times she often had, she was becoming very much aware of the unhappiness which seemed to come into life as unexpectedly as a summer thunderstorm. She herself had been ill in 1840, and at the beginning of that year, Augusta Holmes' father passed away suddenly on a business trip. Mary did her best to comfort her friend.

Albert was more willing than Mary to be resigned to either good or evil as the will of God. He had once written to her:

However far above us, I rely with entire confidence in the justice of God; and whatever may happen to me, for good or for evil, I see the same hand in it all — & seeing it, I can say no less, than that God rules, let the earth submit.

In the New Hampshire legislature Albert was now taking a prominent part in the work of each session. Franklin Pierce had high hopes for this tall, spare young man.[8] Albert's enthusiasm fired others, helping pass needed legislation. His reputation as a speaker spread throughout New Hampshire and into the neighboring state of Massachusetts. It was becoming well known that Albert Baker stood for fairness, justice, and individual rights.

In a letter addressed to both Mary and Martha, he wrote:

If you knew how much satisfaction I take in reading your letters, you would write oftener. . . . Indeed, it is the *oasis* in the desert of life — the only spot upon which I rest with *entire* safety. . . . But my joy was saddened, upon reading in your postscript that Mary's health was again in danger. I pray she will be careful. . . . I go to *Baltimore* the first of May, as one of the Delegates to the convention, and intend to visit you upon my return . . . . Court sits next Tuesday at

Amherst . . . I have some eight or ten *jury trials,* double what I ever
had before. . . . Next Monday, I have engaged to deliver an address
before the "Bay State Association" in *Boston.*

Albert's letters showed his concern for his youngest sister's welfare
and an interest in her growing literary ability. He commented in reference to Mary's recent letters:

In point of literary taste, and skill in execution, I think they excel
any thing I have seen of yours. Be careful that you do not sacrifice
too often at the shrine of the muses. Your health is of paramount
importance, yet, though you may think yourself pretty well. I beg of
you to be careful. I set out for Boston this morning. I am almost worn
out. I have scarcely slept two hours for the last two days.

It was Albert who became seriously ill, and George went to Hillsborough to be with him. Suddenly, in the middle of October, 1841,
Albert passed on. He was only thirty-one and had seemed on the verge
of great achievement. It was a terrible shock to the Baker family. For
Franklin Pierce, who had watched so carefully the rise of his protégé
and friend, this was a personal as well as a political loss.

The newspapers carried remarkable tributes. One paper commented:

His public services . . . are too well known to the people of this state
to require comments. . . . He went emphatically for the greatest good
of the greatest number. He hated tyranny and despised fraud. . . .
His only question was — What is right? and that which in his idea
was the right he would pursue fearless of consequences. . . . His name
will live after him. In his short life he lived long and effected much.[9]

George sorrowfully gathered up Albert's few personal belongings,
his books, his papers, and his letters. These the younger brother kept
through the years until they were handed down to his own son.[10]

For young Mary it was a particularly dark time. Albert had seemed
so bold and assured. She had been so proud of him. She had loved him
the most of all her brothers and sisters.

16

*"In 1843 I was united to my first husband, Colonel George
Washington Glover of Charleston, South Carolina, the ceremony
taking place under the paternal roof in Tilton [Sanbornton]."*
... *Retrospection and Introspection*
MARY BAKER EDDY

Mary was in a somber mood after Albert's death, and it showed in her
writing. The "golden days" of her childhood seemed far away.

Remembering Albert's example, perhaps, and the encouragement
she had been given by the Reverend Mr. Corser and Miss Bodwell, Mary
turned again to thoughts about her education. Abby and Martha had
managed to conclude their schooling. Both had taught school at the
Bridge for a time. Martha, in fact, had been visited by the school committee, which included Mr. Bodwell and Dyer H. Sanborn, and she had
received high commendation for her teaching.[1]

Dyer Sanborn, the Dartmouth graduate who was principal of the
Woodman Academy, had resigned in 1841. He then opened his own
high school. (The term was just beginning to replace that of *academy*.)
Shortly afterward, however, the board of trustees of Sanbornton
Academy, of which Mark Baker was a member, decided to hire Mr.
Sanborn and thereby improve the quality of their school. The Reverend
Mr. Corser was probably grateful to be relieved of his duties as part-
time preceptor; and Dyer Sanborn accepted the trustees' invitation to
become principal of the school on a full-time basis, beginning with the
academic year in 1842.

He took over with a firm hand, bringing the Academy up to standards
that compared favorably with those of the best schools in New England.
Under Mr. Corser there had been but one class of twenty to thirty
students taught by him as preceptor. The year that Dyer Sanborn became
principal, one hundred and two males and seventy-two females were
enrolled. Mary Baker was among them, and despite difficulties with her
health, she completed a full academic year of three terms.

Sanborn himself taught Latin, Greek, and natural science, as it was coming to be known. He employed a staff of assistants, and arranged for thorough instruction in English grammar, with the use of his own textbook. Besides their regular courses, the young ladies took rhetorical exercise and composition every Wednesday afternoon. All except day students were required to spend at least three hours' study in the morning and evening in their rooms.[2]

For Mary, who was now a mature twenty-year-old and thoroughly at home with books, the year must have been a stimulating and happy one. She also had the companionship of a young relative, since brother Samuel's son boarded with the Bakers and attended the Academy.

A number of students Mary's age and older were enrolled at Sanbornton, for many young people were able to conclude their education only after some years of struggle. Among Mary's friends were Martha Rand and Hannah Sanborn. Hannah had attended school with Mary at Tin Corner. John Bartlett, who had been among Mary's first friends in Sanbornton, was still in and out of school as he sought to complete his preparation for Harvard University. The year before, he had attended Dyer Sanborn's high school.

On November 21, 1842, Mary finished her formal schooling. Through persistence she had gained a better than average education. It was a time marked by a number of changes for Mary. Only the day before she left school, her close friend, Augusta Holmes, was married to Samuel Swasey, a former acquaintance of Albert's. Then, three days before Christmas, sister Martha was married to Luther Pilsbury, son of the Bakers' friend Warden Pilsbury. Luther was a deputy warden at the Concord prison.

Mary visited Martha at her new home in Concord soon after the wedding. She described the visit in a letter to Augusta, who was now living in Haverhill, New Hampshire. She found Martha

like yourself believing a lost paradise restored in the 'green bower
of home' while I, unlike his "Satanic Majesty," gaze only to admire
and approve. Really Augusta, you cannot tell how *"doubly lone"*
I feel since you and Martha have gone. I have tried to forget sis, but
Phenix-like her image is constantly rising up before me from some
desolate vestige!

There had been a five-week Methodist revival in town that brought
acquaintances to the Baker home from miles around and apologies from
Mary to Augusta because she could not write. Mary's letter sparkled
with her old exuberance. She referred to the gentleman who taught
penmanship at the Academy:

> . . . the *marvelous* James Smith! Your *crazy correspondent* was
> correct, so far as pretensions warrant; he professes to have religion,
> and so far succeeded in *exhausting* that interesting and exhalted
> subject, I grew weary and retired.

Among others who had "experienced a change" during the revival
was Mary's friend John Bartlett. She underlined his name three times
in her letter, but there was no indication whether the special interest
was Augusta's or her own.

While Mary kept up a running commentary on the young men in
town in her letters, her interest was apparently centering on George
Washington Glover far away in South Carolina. He had visited
Sanbornton once again, evidently in the summer of 1841, arriving one
day in the Bridge unannounced.[3] Mary had come into town on an errand
and thought she saw her brother George. Intending to surprise him, she
slipped up quietly from behind and gave a playful poke, exclaiming,
"Oh, you're dressed up." It was George who turned around — but
George Glover, not Baker! In her flush of embarrassment, Mary probably appeared all the more beautiful to Wash.

Major Glover was tall and handsome, with dark, curly hair and
102   expressive eyes. He was vigorous and sure of himself. He owned a

schooner and several fine horses, and his building enterprises in the South were going well. Only that spring he had written in a bold, carefree vein to George Baker:

I believe among seven builders I am doing one-half of the Business in the City, last Saturday Bills to my workmen was $1267.00. . . . I shall dine at the Alhambra East Bay Street. I will drink your health and success.[4]

After the visit Mary had pasted in her scrapbook a little reading of George Glover's personality by a phrenologist, a person who claimed to be able to tell character by the shape of one's head. The phrenologist had written: "naturally cheerful and fond of enterprise, yet too cautious to venture much himself, without he is sure of success!" Mary wrote beside it "in proof thereof Sept. 5-1841."

At some time after Major Glover's return to Charleston, he must have determined to assure his success so far as Mary was concerned. When his correspondence became more regular, Mark Baker was troubled. Possibly Mark was unsure that George Glover was the best choice for Mary. In any event, South Carolina seemed a strange land to him. He worried that the courtship might lead to marriage and eventually to Mary's going away to live in an "unhealthy" climate. At some point early in 1843, he began to intercept Wash's weekly letters.

Mary believed, of course, that the letters had suddenly stopped, and painfully imagined all sorts of reasons for this. But brother George was not so naïve. He took his sister aside and expressed the opinion that their father was intercepting the letters.

George had great regard for Wash Glover, and he could not bear to see Mary's distress. He conceived the plan of taking Mary along on his forthcoming business trip to the White Mountains. He wrote to Wash, informing him of their route and the hotels where they would stop. With any luck at all, Wash's letters would finally get through.

To Mark, the trip seemed plausible enough, and he supposed that it might even be helpful to Mary's health.

The brother and sister stopped the first night at a hotel in Thornton. Martha, who may have understood the real reason for the trip, had sent a nosegay of flowers along, and Mary wrote in her journal that evening:

Dear Martha's nosegay is withered. I have carried it in my hand from S— and have not needed her monitor to jog my memory.[5]

In her room Mary felt pensive and lonely. She wondered whether she would really have any letters from the South after all. She wrote in her journal:

The lonely night-wind sighs a dull requiem to my spirits the rain is pelting the windows and I am thinking of home and *thee*. During today's ride we passed some beautiful spots, beautiful to the passer-by but not the *home for me*.

The next night in her room at the Notch House, Mary's spirits were still low, but she could not help appreciating the beauty of the view from her window.

Oh! what a scene is spread out before me. The gigantic hills in slumbering beauty seem from their cloud-capped summits as if in communion with Heaven. . . . O that I was a bird . . . to look upon the lower regions in their vast insignificance . . . to contemplate all in God and God *in all*.

She jotted down a note about the Old Man of the Mountain, a famous rock formation she had seen that day:

And a *rock-bound* sire he is, upon a ragged cliff beyond the reach of mortal! Stern and passionless, his rigid features betray *no soul* — tho they present from one point a complete profile of the human face.

Then she hastily concluded: "Dear bro' Geo has come in to tell me I must retire."

Another day "wandered into the ocean of eternity," and then it

must have come — the letter, or letters, from Wash Glover. Her spirits soared. "Never," she wrote, "have I enjoyed a ride as much since I left home as the one this morning with Geo. from Franconia to Littleton; and from thence to Haverhill alone." Suddenly Mary felt "in much better health and spirits than I have before for a long time. . . . We left behind the whole panorama of mountain scenery clad with vapors, magnificient, and alone!" She ate "voraciously" at lunch, and later described the trip to Haverhill in a lively letter to George:

Since I left you I have made it a religious duty to obey you in *all things.* . . . I reached here about 6 o'clock P.M. was the only passenger inside, and such a *sky-rocket* adventure I never had; some times I really thought I was at least *midway* between heaven and earth, till the driver's shrill whistle, or a more tolerable road would restore my senses; Mr. Hale is the very most polite good natured driver in the *whole world* (as *I have seen it all*) and was very kind to me on your account I suppose.

At Haverhill, Mary was met "by my old friend *Augusta* (alias *Mrs. Swasey*) with a loud laugh and a hearty kiss." The two young women talked until the small hours of the morning about, one may be sure, the coming event that was so soon to change Mary's life entirely.

By Thanksgiving, the Bakers were becoming resigned to the idea that the youngest daughter would marry Wash Glover. Mary had always been the object of their special love and concern. They had watched over her closely because she seemed so delicate, and now she was being taken far away. Who would care for her if she became ill? It was some ninety-five hours from Concord to Charleston. For the Bakers it might as well have been the other side of the world.

In his efforts to keep Wash Glover's letters from Mary, Mark had not, in his own sight, been acting unjustly. He was simply deeply concerned about his daughter, and his wife, for once, had sided with him. However, the family put aside their forebodings for the time being. The Thanksgiving holiday had always been a very special one for them, and they wanted this last Thanksgiving together to be remembered happily by Mary. They assembled around Mrs. Baker's festive table, loaded with turkey, mince pies, plum puddings — traditional New England fare.

George handed Mary a poem that spoke for them all:

Say Sister,
Why that tear o'er youth's fair cheek,
To scald its hope flushed glow
Why shrinks that heart in sadness deep
Which joys of youth should only know
Thy bark though frail the bark of life
May safely mount the swelling tide
Whilst sterling worth and pious aim
Anchor and helm — with thee abide
When tossed o'er life's tempestuous sea
If virtue still shall brace the sail
Safely moored thy bark shall be
At close of day — and calm the gale.

Mary then replied:

Brother, the thoughts of childhood free
Throng in my 'wildered brain
Remember, O remember me
Till I come back again.
Sisters, in woman's gentle heart
Affection loves to dwell
I'll wrong thee not to *ask my part*
Beloved ones all farewell.[6]

George W. Glover of Charleston, South Carolina, and Mary M. Baker of Sanbornton were married on Sunday, December 10, 1843. The ceremony was performed in the parlor of the Baker home by the Reverend Corban Curtice. Mary wrote of it simply and eloquently years later: "I married young the one I loved." [7]

Friends, neighbors, and relatives crowded the farmhouse, their sleighs and horses filling the yard. George was there, Samuel with his wife and children, and Abby and Martha with their husbands. Mark and Abigail Baker rejoiced to have the entire family assembled, though their happiness was shadowed by their anxiety about Mary. They tried not to let it show; and at last Mr. and Mrs. George Washington Glover were sped on their way with shouts of congratulation and good wishes.

The newlyweds drove first to Concord, where they visited friends. Then they traveled to Bow along the familiar turnpike. Mary wanted to say good-bye to the homestead and the fields and woods that had meant so much to her. Afterwards they took the Boston train from Concord. The first locomotive, the Amoskeag, had come chugging into town the year before pulling three passenger cars. Now trains ran three times daily.

In Boston, Mr. and Mrs. Glover boarded the ship that was to take them south. The odor of tar and hemp mingled with the fresh salt breeze as they went to their cabin. Commands rang out, the rigging creaked, sails were hoisted; and slowly they moved into the harbor past ships from all parts of the globe. To Mary it was like setting sail for a new continent.

17

"After parting with the dear home circle I went with him [her husband] to the South; but he was spared to me for only one brief year. . . . A month later I returned to New Hampshire, where, at the end of four months, my babe was born."
. . . Retrospection and Introspection
MARY BAKER EDDY

The city of Charleston presented a beautiful appearance as the Glovers' ship made port. It was one of the elegant cities of America, known as the Queen City of the South. There were gracious, brick buildings in the southern style, with lacy wrought-iron balconies. The wide streets were lined with magnolia trees. The air was mild even in January — different, indeed, from Sanbornton and Concord.

Shortly after their arrival, Mary and George moved to Wilmington, North Carolina, where George had business interests. There Mrs. Glover immediately became absorbed in her husband's activities. Wash was well known and well liked, a member of the Masonic order. His wife was quickly included in his circle of friends. Some of Mary's special interests readily found an outlet. She had always followed politics closely because of her devotion to Albert and his career, and now at the request of the candidate for governor of the state she wrote the toasts for one of the Democratic dinners.[1]

Abigail Baker had found it difficult to part with her youngest child. Her letters to Mary were full of longing to see her, to go to church with her, just to hear her voice in the house. In her letters, Abigail sometimes pretended she was able to stop by for a visit. She wrote:

And now Mary I will visit you in your own Room at your fireside with dear George are you happy as you anticipated; is your room furnished agreeable to your mind?

The mother's letters brought tidbits of news and questions about the climate and Mary's health, jotted down in brief moments between household tasks. Abigail described one of the family's evenings:

Martha is much engaged in sewing . . . we wish you were here to assist her . . . we miss your good Cheer I look out the window and say how I wish I could see George and Mary coming over the hill.

In a letter written several months later, Abigail was able to include some especially good news. Martha, who had returned with her husband to Connecticut, had given birth to a "little fat beautiful Daughter" named Ellen.

Mary was still pursuing her literary career. She wrote for one of the newspapers, contributing at least one review of a local dramatic production.[2] A new magazine for women, called *The Floral Wreath,* had been established in South Carolina, and Mary was among its first contributors. Not surprisingly, she chose to write about New Hampshire. One of her poems was on the Old Man of the Mountain, which she had seen on her trip to the White Mountains the year before. George was in the midst of plans for his most ambitious project — the building of a cathedral in Haiti. The young couple discussed the trip in detail, and Mary wrote a verse describing her feelings on preparing to leave for the West Indies.

But suddenly George was stricken with fever. All plans were swept away. Even the lumber for the Haiti project was lost.[3] The doctor in attendance and George's friends in the Masonic lodge were deeply concerned about the young wife, who was soon to become a mother. Mary prayed without ceasing, remembering her own childhood experience of the healing of a fever and her mother's frequent assurances that "God is able to raise you up from sickness." Why, she wondered in her anguish, was there no change in her husband's condition? Why could not her prayers aid him?

After nine days of illness, George passed on, and Mary was left brokenhearted, hundreds of miles from home.[4] She had become a wife and widow in the span of only half a year. Wash's friends rallied to help, and one of the Masons was chosen to make the long journey with her to New York.

The trip home from the South in the oppressive heat of July was a torturous experience for the expectant mother. Mary recorded in her journal the weariness of "traveling in four days and nights . . . the distance of about fourteen hundred miles," with constant changes from "cars" to steamboat to ferryboat to "cars." Brother George met her in New York.[5]

Her health was very poor after the grueling journey, but her child, named for her husband and her brother George, was born safely in September. For some time, however, she could not take care of him, and finally, her father took Georgy to the home of a woman who could nurse the baby. For long hours Mark sat by Mary's bed. The family felt that she might not live. Sister Abby was unable to help because after the birth of her son Albert she too had fallen ill.

Mary's recovery was very slow.[6] She did not gain much relief from medicines, and she may have begun to question at this time why some people recovered more quickly than others. It may have been then that she first began to trace a relationship between physical illness and a mental cause.[7]

Despite her most earnest prayers, the young mother did not become well enough to take the full responsibility of caring for her son. As Georgy grew strong and high-spirited like his father, there were days when Mary was simply too ill to look after him. Mahala Sanborn, who often helped in the Baker home and was like one of the family, had cared for Mary when she was critically ill. She was fond of Georgy, and she seemed the obvious one to take the child when later he proved too much for the household to handle.

During Mary's absence in the South, George Baker had been gaining prominence in local affairs. He had been made an aide-de-camp to the governor and he held several offices in the town, among them that of prudential committeeman or member of the finance committee for the school district.[8] George joined the school district supervising committee one day on a visit to a class taught by Mary's friend Martha Rand. The committee gave a glowing report, and thereafter George's letters made frequent mention of Mathy Rand.

Mathy gave up her teaching to continue her education at the New Hampshire Conference Seminary, founded in 1845 to replace Sanbornton Academy. The Seminary was a venture well financed by the Methodist Episcopal Church, and was considered an excellent school for many years. Mary's friend John Bartlett also enrolled. Like the Academy before it, the Seminary offered a combination of high school and college courses.[9]

Shortly after the founding of the school, the Reverend Richard Rust, an outstanding young educator, became its principal. He was about Mary's age and well known to the Baker family. He had a fine voice and often joined Mary and her brother George, Mathy Rand, and John Bartlett in their sings. Caroline Lane, preceptress at the Seminary, and William Sleeper (known as "Sleeper"), later principal of Woodman Academy, were also included in these singing get-togethers. These friends were undoubtedly a great comfort to the young widow as she struggled to put the pieces of her life together in a new pattern.

Richard Rust noticed Mary's natural ability to teach, and on one occasion prevailed upon her to substitute for a short time at the Conference Seminary. Mary handled the job so capably that he urged her to go on teaching in some form not so taxing as the district schools or academies. Her Sunday School class had been a great success, so she naturally thought of a school for small children. Her health was slightly improved, Abby was willing to help, and all concerned must have felt that Mary's life might finally be taking a calmer and pleasanter course.

The Tiltons permitted the use of a small building on their property. They had it painted red and fitted with small tables and chairs. Mary's school began with an enrollment of forty children. Today it would be considered a typical nursery school or kindergarten, but in that era it was a distinct novelty.

Mrs. Glover's school attracted considerable attention. She did not neglect discipline, but substituted love for harshness whenever possible. Even more revolutionary than this was her belief that if knowledge could be made truly interesting, children would naturally want it.

Years later, one little girl, Sarah Clement, recalled her teacher's kindness and cheerfulness. In the evening, on those days when Mary stayed at the Tiltons' home, the child, who was a neighbor, would run across the street, climb the gate, and watch Mrs. Glover work in the garden. Mary loved a garden and flowers and managed nearly all her life to have one no matter where she lived.

Sarah remembered that one day she had been very naughty in school. Finally, after several admonitions, Mrs. Glover sent her outside to bring a switch from the garden. Sarah looked about until she found the smallest twig. She presented this gravely to the teacher, who thereupon lost all her dignity, burst into laughter, and sent the young culprit back to her seat, unpunished.

Mary's experiment with the kindergarten was short-lived. The uncertainty of her health made regular teaching a trial, and of course there was her own Georgy to care for. She was finally forced to give up the school.

Now she proudly turned to her writing to help support herself. Several of her pieces had been published in *The Floral Wreath* after her husband's death. She now sent poems and articles to *The Covenant,* a magazine published by the Odd Fellows organization. One of her poems was accepted by the *Freemason's Monthly* and several others by the *New Hampshire Patriot.* The income was very small, though, and not nearly enough to provide a home for Georgy.

In 1846 Abby lost a son a few weeks after birth, and Mary did whatever she could to help her older sister. For some time afterwards with her mother's help she took care of Abby's boy. The two cousins, now between two and three years old, must have made a considerable commotion in the Baker home, and they probably taxed the strength of all concerned.

Mr. Curtice, the Congregational minister who had replaced Mr. Corser, called regularly on the family, and Mary coached the youngsters to act with decorum for these visits. She would make believe that she was the minister and intone with dignity, as the boys stood at polite attention, such questions as, "Come here, little boy, what is your name, and where do you come from, and what do you do?" Albert would invariably recite at top speed the needed information, but Georgy would inevitably interrupt, "Too fast, Albert, too fast!" However, when Mr. Curtice did call, the results were apparently quite satisfactory.

At this period, friction seems to have developed between the Tiltons and George Baker. The Tilton and Baker mill was sold to another company, though Alexander Tilton continued to occupy the building under lease. He installed new machinery, and the Tilton Mills continued with immense success. George, who had decided to try his fortunes in New York, left Sanbornton in October, 1847. Mary missed him greatly as he had been such a help in the handling of her son.

She spent much time now with her sister Abby. But whenever she brought Georgy to the Tilton home, he was sent to play at Mahala Sanborn's. Possibly because Abby had lost one child, she had fears for her son Albert. Georgy was a boisterous youngster, while Albert was turning out to be quite a delicate child.

Mary's health was a little better, Mrs. Baker reported to George in December, 1847. The young mother was writing much of the time, with Georgy constantly at her elbow. She found great joy in being with him whenever she was able. Mary wrote in one of her poems:

O' heaven-born task, to watch thy dawning mind
Each day's development of ripening thought —
To sit and see almost the twig inclined,
The pliant sapling form the sturdy oak.[10]

She would sit and rock Georgy, watching him fall asleep. Often the tears would come to her eyes as she considered her helpless situation and her inability to care for him. She recalled later that one day as she rocked the child gently back and forth, a big tear fell on his cheek. He wakened, reached up with his little hand to touch her face, and murmured, "Mama not lonesome. Georgy is company. Georgy's not 'sleep." Then, promptly, he fell back to sleep again.

Among the articles Mary wrote during this period was an essay on the "Immortality of the Soul." Her keen thought was restless and searching, though her Bible was her guide and constant companion. As in her childhood, she could not be satisfied with anything less than exploring a question thoroughly for herself. She had been concerned with precision of language since the time spent with the Lindley Murray *Readers*, and in this particular essay on immortality, she discussed the need for a language that would better express the things of the spirit. Wondering about the state of man in eternity, she asked, "Will the mind be continually augmenting its stock of knowledge, and advancing toward complete perfection?" She answered, "It cannot be otherwise," and continued:

The imperfection of language will be no hindrance to the acquisition of ideas, as it will no longer be necessary as a medium of thought and communication. Intelligence, refined, etherealized, will converse directly with material objects, if, indeed, matter be existent. All will be accessible, permanent, eternal!¹¹

But much of what Mary wrote was of necessity in the journalistic style of the day. She was writing to earn money as well as to express herself. Thus she produced a novelette in four chapters called "Emma Clinton, A Tale of the Frontier," which capitalized on the growing interest in the West; a short story named "The Test of Love"; an essay advocating Irish freedom; and many short poems. All of these efforts were accepted and published.

There were times now when she was depressed by ill health and a seeming lack of direction. She had answered decisively as a child when asked what she wanted to do. But she was not writing a book now, nor did she seem to be moving ahead with certainty.

The family helped as best they could. She had been taken to the White Mountains for another trip by George and she accompanied

Alexander Tilton on a trip to Boston to help choose some elegant furniture for the Tilton home. She was still a young woman and enthusiastic and energetic in her thought, even though constantly hampered by physical weakness. She wrote to her sister Martha in March of 1848: "I feel as if I must *begin* something this summer, if my health is sufficient. I am weary working my way through life from the *middle* to the *end.*" In a letter written later in the same month, Mary poured out her heart to her friend Mathy Rand:

Now dearest Mathy . . . I have half determined this very moment to throw aside my pen and wait to *weep.* But then what availeth this mood . . . 'tis like looking down through the transparent waters of the sea of life, checkered with sunshine and shade — into the mighty deep, in which our happier days have sunk, and where they are lying still visible like golden sands; and half in hope grasp after them again, then draw back the hand, filled only with briny tears! . . . . But forgive this strain of melancholy, and I will try for your sake to rally my spirits in a lighter and more *brief* exposition.[12]

Then, having given expression to these melancholy feelings, she went on in a girlish way to mention some of the local talk about the townspeople. In referring to the departure of John Bartlett for his last term at Harvard, she hoped that now people would "mind their business about either of us, as I am getting a little *mad* at their *lies,* for such they are." She had said earlier in her letter to her sister Martha that "I *shall not marry* any one I know at *present* — the future however may do better by me in this respect."

Nevertheless Mary had become increasingly fond of this friend whom she had known since she was sixteen. There was much of Albert Baker in John Bartlett. He had a disciplined mind and a drive that kept him moving towards his goal. Despite Mary's protests, there were indications that she had more than a passing interest in the young man.

She expressed her own philosophy concerning the future as she closed her letter to Mathy Rand with the advice:

You must not feel sad or anxious about the future . . . let us ever remember, there is One "who careth for us" — too wise to err, too *good* to be unkind. On Him you may rely, and find a Father and a friend. Yes, dear Mathy, this is my only consolation, *unworthy* as I am — and 'tis the greatest I can recommend to those I love.

18

"The night before my child was taken from me, I knelt by his side throughout the dark hours, hoping for a vision of relief from this trial."

. . . *Retrospection and Introspection*
MARY BAKER EDDY

Mary had seen something of the world beyond the Bridge, and at times she longed to return to the South. Many other young people in the spring of 1848 were yearning to go west. The frontier had been opening up rapidly, but that winter gold was discovered in California. Now the race to the "golden West" was on! By ship around "the Horn," and overland by wagon train, thousands flocked to San Francisco and Sacramento to seek their fortunes in the gold fields. It was said one could make ten to fifty dollars a day merely by gathering the precious nuggets and dust from rivers and streams. Martha's husband, Luther Pilsbury, ventured westward along with thousands of other New England men. Mary wrote her sister, "My heart aches for you and Luther both, to be separated as you have been."

In the same letter Mary confessed, "I want to learn to play on a piano so I can go south and teach. Tis all I shall ever be *able* to do, and this *once* accomplished and I am independent." However, she confided to her sister that their father could not see the necessity for purchasing a piano. He was planning to build a new house in town, and Mary concluded, "Tis vain I expect for me [to] *try now*. Still I shall do something next Summer, *what* I know not."

Martha was evidently trying to arrange somehow to help the youngest sister, and Mary wrote her:

God bless you for such kindness. . . . My tears are falling on my
cheeks as I say it; but Martha, I am weary of this world, it has *no*
joy for me. . . . I dont know what to write of news; as I so seldom go
out — and Geo being gone, I hear nothing; have spent but one week
with Sis this winter.

Then, as in her letter to Mathy Rand, Mary was able to jump from a note of despondency to one of gaiety. She was just too full of life to sink into despair. She possessed a natural buoyancy and a determination to express it that kept her afloat in spite of sadness and ill health:

There has been some sleigh ridding — and because of the license of
Leap Year *I* and *Miss Lane,* the Sem. Teacher and Miss Rand invited
our *Driver* and took a ride to Concord! after driving, returned to
Loudon; supped, then came home, had a real *spree with ourselves*
no Gents. Made the driver (Sleeper) foot the bill and laugh at the
joke. What do you think of this? Wasn't it *genteel?*

Mary spoke happily, also, of the hope that Martha and her child Nell might come to Sanbornton for a visit:

Yes, indeed, — Abi and I seldom meet without mentioning it. . . .
Oh! Mat, to see the three beautiful children meet . . . must it not
give to the *Mothers'* hearts a joy. . . . Little Geo. is very good and
very *naughty,* not subject to any judicious discipline. He loves you
and Nell most dearly. I think he will remember you when he sees
you; he identifies Nell with every little girl he sees; kiss her a thousand times for us both. Mum. wants very much to see you both;
as *do we all* . . . .

Ever yr. loving &
faithful Sis, M.

Abby and her husband were becoming more and more prominent in business and social circles.[1] Abby apparently had some hand in urging Mark to buy a lot near the Tilton house and build a fine new home. She wished, perhaps, that her father could give a more prosperous impression to her friends. Mother Baker, however, was not well and not looking forward with enthusiasm to the move into the Bridge which her husband was planning. Nor was Mary really interested in the move. Her one desire was to free herself from depending on her family.

John Bartlett was now definitely Mary's suitor, and as summer approached and she considered the future, she made up her mind.[2] Even though John would need several years before he became an established lawyer, he had the prospect of a promising career. The young man had known Georgy since birth, and Mary felt she could count on his love for her son.

In August, 1848, Mary Glover journeyed to Cambridge to see John Bartlett graduate from Harvard Law School. He had made a brilliant record for himself. Now he awaited Mary's decision. It was "yes." No immediate plans were made for the marriage, however. John, like others, had been stirred by the popular slogan, "Ho, for California," and wanted to go west. He would go by way of Illinois to seek his and Mary Glover's fortune in the land of gold.

Mrs. Baker wrote of Mary to George, "I think her mind is fully established." But about herself she commented unhappily:

Dear George, I feel as thoug my glass was almost run. . . . I must say that every line from you is a *Luxury* except when you begin about *Fate* that's a great word and it distres's me for I know too well how to sympathise with you.

Mrs. Baker's letters revealed a certain sadness and sense of failure. She had worked so diligently at the rearing of her children. Of them all, only Mary seemed to share her mother's spirituality. And now what was happening to this life that Abigail had felt was dedicated to the special service of God? Was Mary doomed to be an invalid? The mother and daughter attended the church meetings and prayer meetings which they had enjoyed so much together before Mary's departure for the South. And Abigail perhaps prayed more fervently to know God's will.

Later in the year, Mary became so ill again that the Bakers sent her to the town of Warner, twenty-five miles away, for medical treatment. On the eve of George's birthday, Abigail wrote him that she was thinking back sadly to the children's early days:

I have given full scope to recollection and I find the retrospect of departed years afford but little *Solid* satisfaction yet when I reflect and remember the days when our Family Circle were composed of six Children with tallents (pardon me) and voices sufficient to raise a Mothers heart to Heaven I feel to thank God for what he has done for them but O how have we all perverted our tallents. I feel for one to humble myself daily before God and ask his forgiveness.

She added, with a touch of Biblical phrasing:

This may be the last Caution I Ever give you and be not Angry with me if I say Touch not, Taste not, neither use a Profane word; for you are Bought with a price and Precious and my Love abideth with you Ever.

Abigail did not live to move into the new house.[3] George returned home early in November of 1849 to marry Mathy Rand, and the couple left immediately for Baltimore. Mrs. Baker passed on several weeks after the ceremony. A newspaper tribute to her commented fittingly that "her life was a living illustration of Christian faith."

The day her mother passed away Mary sat down sadly to tell George and Mathy in Baltimore:

She has suffered long with me let me then be willing she should now rejoice and I bear on till I follow her. I cannot write more my grief overpowers me.

It was only a few weeks following her mother's death, that word came to Mary from California: John Bartlett had died in Sacramento.

He had survived the perilous overland journey only to pass on shortly after his arrival.[4] The winter in which Mother Baker and John Bartlett passed away was a dreary one for Mary and her father. After some forty years of marriage, Mark missed his wife's presence deeply. He wrote George apologizing for his penmanship, explaining he had been in such poor health since Abigail's death that his hand trembled.[5] Mary wrote to George later in the year telling how she

went into that cold, damp [new] house with father, helped cleanse and set it in order and lived alone with a little [hired] girl and him all winter; in the spring he told me if George was not sent away he would send him to the *poor house.*

Georgy, now six years old, was spending more time with Mahala Sanborn, for Mary was often confined to bed. At the Sanborns', Georgy was allowed to do nearly as he pleased. Mahala's father let him run free in his blacksmith shop, a wonderfully intriguing place for a small boy. And Mahala, a motherly person, now in her forties and still unmarried, tended to spoil the boy with her lavish affection.

The habits Georgy learned at the Sanborns', added to his already boisterous nature, must have made him a trial to his grandfather. Mark at this time had the responsibility not only for Mary and Georgy but also for Martha and her two daughters, since Martha's husband, Luther Pilsbury, had passed on suddenly on a western trip, in October, 1850. For a little while, the sisters and their children were together.[6] Then Martha left to stay with her late husband's relatives. It was a sad contrast to the joyous reunion Mary had visualized in her letter several years before.[7]

When Mahala Sanborn announced her forthcoming marriage to Russell Cheney, who lived in North Groton, a mountain village about forty miles to the north of Sanbornton, she indicated that she wanted to take Georgy with her. Suddenly, perhaps, Abby and Mark saw this as a solution to the difficult problem of caring for the boy.

Mark had decided to remarry and felt he could no longer have Mary and her son living with him. It was not unusual for a husband to marry only a few months after the passing of his wife, and Mark had waited a year. His new wife was to be the well-to-do widow of a prominent family in nearby Londonderry. Her name was Elizabeth Patterson Duncan.

When Mrs. Duncan's best carpets and furnishings began arriving to replace those that had belonged to Mother Abigail, Mark asked Mary to arrange them. The task was more than she could bear. She flatly refused to help. She was still as high-spirited and determined as her father, and the new arrangement seemed to her a sacrilege.

While Abby was willing to offer her sister a home, she refused to include Georgy. The child, she said, must go with Mahala to North Groton. It was not that the older sister was cold hearted. Usually a sister, brother, or niece was living with her. But her own health was poor at the time, she was concerned over the welfare of her child, and Georgy must have seemed more than her generosity could bear.

Mary could not believe that her sister and father were serious when they first discussed the plan. But her pleas were in vain, and Abby and Mark were unyielding. They were convinced that their plan was the most practical solution. The difficulty was that Mary could offer no reasonable alternative. Finally she consented, but in her heart she must have cherished the thought that even though she let the child go now, it would be possible to get him back later. She knew that Mahala would take good care of him and that the boy was fond of her. But she herself would work hard at her writing or open a school or somehow make enough money to support her son!

While Mahala was getting settled in North Groton, Georgy was sent on a visit to Concord, where he stayed with his Uncle Andrew, Wash Glover's brother. Mary wrote from the Tiltons' when it was time for the boy to return home:

Sanbornton Bridge April 22

My dear Bro and Sis,

Mrs. Cheney came here last Thurs. and will return next week on
Saturday. You can send my dear child when you please, the
latter part of the week, as she is very anxious to have him when
she goes home. She is very fond of children and Georgy in
particular, but her health is very poor, this I regret. She told
me their school (which is about one quarter of a mile distant)
will commence in a few weeks and I am anxious to have him
attend. But Oh! how I *miss him* already! There seems nothing left
me now to enjoy. I often stand by my window when the shades
of evening close o'er me and gaze on yonder sacred spot
where sleeps my peaceful *Mother* and invoke her blessing and
counsel, while I almost envy her repose. But I must not write
on this subject for words are impotent things to utter the
feelings of a *Mother's* heart.

Wont you send me a line by him or come yourselves? I want
very much to know how you have succeeded with him and if he
has been a good boy (some naughty things of course) there is no
child whom we expect mature in every respect, but take Georgy
with the aggregate, is he not a pretty good and very dear boy?
You can speak to the conductor to take care of him and his
little baggage and Mr. Tilton is always at the depot so he will
see to him there. Will dear little Sully be sorry to have him leave?
How is Fath and Moth's health? Give much love to them from
me and accept the same yourselves. Kiss the little one for me
and tell him aunty remembers those roguish eyes. In much haste
Yours Affectionately,

Mary

When Georgy returned from Concord to her outstretched arms,
Mary's heart faltered at the plan. How could she part with him? The
night before he was taken away, she prayed by his bedside until day-
break.[8] Why . . . oh why? she must have wondered in her grief. In the
end, she helped dress the child and packed his clothes. As she tenderly
folded each small garment, she wept. Could this be God's will — to take

"...words are impotent things to utter the feelings of a Mother's heart."
The Farmhouse, Old Sturbridge Village

a child from his mother? She wrote in her journal on May 9, 1851, the day Georgy left:

Go little voyager, o'er life's rough sea —
Born in a tempest! choose thy pilot God,
The Bible, let thy chart forever be —
Anchor and helm its promises afford.

Could monarch's diadem or lordly crown
Or oriental treasures purchase thee?
Ah! 'twere a mockery, 'twere a paltry sum
Coined for so bright a gem as little G.

Grief and suffering for Mary Baker Glover now seemed to be a raging fire consuming every hope. The golden days of her childhood, the sense of God's love and closeness, seemed almost lost. Yet in later years Mary would be able to write:

Sorrow has its reward. It never leaves us where it found us. The furnace separates the gold from the dross that the precious metal may be graven with the image of God.'

"My dominant thought in marrying again was to get back my child, but after our marriage his stepfather was not willing he should have a home with me."

... *Retrospection and Introspection*
MARY BAKER EDDY

19

Mary seemed unable to rise above the waves of despair that came as she watched Georgy depart. Where, she must have wondered, was the God she had known as a child? Why were her most earnest prayers not answered? Her old ailments returned and new complications were added, plunging her into an illness so severe that Abby sent for Martha, who had been staying with relatives.

Martha rushed to the Tilton home in Sanbornton. Here, she reported to George and Mathy, she found Mary "confined to the room and bed except when possibly able to be helped into a carriage to ride." She continued:

> To witness the agony she often endures . . . pierces a sister's heart.
> . . . I am quite worn out and sick, and have come up to Father's to
> try rest with a little medicine. . . . But have we not the assurance,
> and can *I* ever doubt it, that "as thy day so shall thy strength be."
> May mine continue that I may contribute to dear Mary's comfort
> while she may live, if she cannot recover, and afford Abby the
> assistance she so much needs.

Tenderhearted Martha nursed Mary constantly, pouring out her love in an effort that finally began to bring results. The stepmother did her part. Martha told George that she was a "most affectionate person. . . . We all love her very much." [1] As if to make up for his youngest daughter's sorrow, Mr. Baker spent hours sitting with her. He carried her out to the Tiltons' carriage as she began to gain strength, and the three sisters sometimes drove quietly about the countryside together.

Martha bought a small house and set up housekeeping for herself and her children. Her oldest girl, Ellen, was eight, and Mary Neal, who was named for Aunt Mary, was three. The little girl would often sit by her aunt's bedside, quietly visiting with her. Mary loved the children, though their presence gave her moments of sadness as she thought of her own separation from Georgy.

But little by little, Mary began to rally. She had not lost her wit and her interest in life. Franklin Pierce, Albert's friend, had been elected President of the United States, and Mary wrote a sonnet about him which was published in the *New Hampshire Patriot* in October, 1852.

Now in her early thirties, Mary retained her attractiveness in spite of the trials she had been through. Dr. Daniel Patterson, a dentist in the town of Franklin, New Hampshire, could not help noticing this particular patient. He became more and more taken with her, and when she wrote asking for an appointment, he took the occasion to open correspondence.

Dr. Patterson was a tall man, strong and handsome, with a flowing beard. He was a dandy in his manner of dressing, given to wearing varnished boots and a silk top hat. More than once in his life Daniel Patterson would mix vague hopes for the best and a certain amount of carelessness — with disastrous results! He was impetuous and warm-hearted, sincere so far as he was able to be. His pleading of his cause to Mary was carried on in high-sounding, windy letters.[2]

Mary was thirty-one and Daniel thirty-four. She found Daniel a likable companion, but most important, he seemed to be the means for at last establishing a home for Georgy.

Dr. Patterson professed a desire not only to marry Mrs. Glover but to take her boy as well. At one point, he assured the family that he felt Mary's health would be restored as soon as Georgy was returned to her. He proposed formally in March, 1853, but was rejected. The reason, according to Mary's letters, was her concern about Dr. Patterson's religious views. She wrote Daniel, "I have a fixed feeling that to yield my *religion* to yours, I *could not,* other things compared to this, are but a grain to the universe."[3]

Possibly Mark's influence had swayed Mary's decision. In any event, his strong hand was apparent in still another objection to marriage which Mary passed along to her suitor. "Dark things" about Dr. Patterson's character had been heard.

Daniel was not one to yield to such a charge. He sent back letters expressing his wounded feelings and sweeping protestations of his innocence. His campaign was eventually a success. He convinced all concerned that there could be no reasonable objection to his desire to make Mary his wife. The family, of course, was not hardhearted about the separation of Mary and her child. They were anxious for a solution, and this may have led to their yielding of original, more accurate intuitions.

After the wedding in June, 1853, Dr. and Mrs. Patterson took an apartment in the adjoining town of Franklin. Later Dr. Patterson purchased a modest house on the bank of a river, near the headwaters of the Merrimack which Mary had known as a child in Bow. How she enjoyed having her own place again, putting it in the exact order in which she always took such pleasure. She once said that she was not patient with a speck of dirt. She was a good housewife, thanks to her mother's training, and a good cook, though in this period of her life she had to rely mainly on others.

Unfortunately, Mary's joy in her new home soon began to dim. It appeared that Dr. Patterson was not going to accept her son as he had promised. His argument was that her health was not yet good enough to bear up under caring for a husky nine-year-old.

In the course of his dental practice, Dr. Patterson was often away. There were few in the profession, and it was customary for dentists to travel from town to town. Thus there were many days when Mary Baker Patterson was alone while her husband journeyed about the countryside. She would sometimes sit on the bank of the river as she had as a child, watching the swiftly flowing water tumble over the rocks on its way towards Bow. The scene of the golden days of her childhood was far to the south. Her child, so dear to her, was far to the north.

The lines of one of the great hymns she was to write years later would reflect the depth of her feelings. Its words could have been a poignant prayer for her own child — and for all children. "Thou Love that guards the nestling's faltering flight!" she wrote, "Keep Thou my child on upward wing tonight." [4]

Mary was becoming thoroughly convinced that Dr. Patterson had no intention of making a place for Georgy in their home. It is possible that the doctor realized he had simply undertaken more than he could manage. He seems never to have been in a sound financial condition, despite the fact that he was adept at dentistry and it was a profession which generally paid well.

In December of 1855 the Tilton mill burned to the ground, causing a large financial loss to Abby and her husband.[5] With the enterprise that had made the undertaking a success in the first place, the couple began to rebuild the business.

The year before, a daughter was born to Abby, and the oldest sister had another setback in health. For the rest of her life, there is mention of her poor health in family letters. However, like Mary, she showed a determination not to give in to illness.

Earlier Dr. Patterson might have counted on help from his wealthy in-laws, but now the destruction of the Tilton mill forestalled even hinting for such assistance. In desperation over the hopelessness of the situation, Mary appealed to her sister Martha.[6] As always, the middle sister did what she could. In this case it was a great deal! She loaned Dr. Patterson the money to finance what Mary yearned for. In the spring of 1855, Mary and Dr. Patterson were able to move to North Groton to be near Georgy.

Martha's financial situation was not such that she could easily afford the generous loan. However, the Tiltons and the Bakers must have been still confident in the doctor's ability to repay, or they would not have permitted Martha to assist him. With the loan, Dr. Patterson purchased a house and land in North Groton which gave him part interest in a sawmill. The house was near the main road beside a mountain stream. One of the Pattersons' neighbors was the town postmaster, and another the local blacksmith. Georgy lived not far away with Mahala and her husband.

With great hope, Mary reestablished her relationship with her son. They had been apart for almost four years, and Georgy was now eleven years old. Eagerly his mother asked the boy to bring his school books to her. Four years before, when Georgy had been taken away, she had bravely resisted the desire to cling to him. She had sent him on his way promptly, so he could be enrolled at the beginning of the school term.

Now, she hoped to see much improvement in his education. To her sorrow, she found it was being neglected. Mahala, like many others of the period, looked lightly upon schooling.

Mary helped Daniel Kidder, a neighbor's son, with his schoolwork. It was obviously natural for her to set about at once to remedy the situation in regard to Georgy. But her efforts met with resistance. After four years away, Georgy seemed moody and behaved inconsistently.

Mahala had not shared the boy for some time, and she may have found it hard to do so now, especially when the mother was critical of his education — or lack of it. Dr. Patterson found Georgy one more annoyance in what had become to him a trying situation, perhaps feeling the restrictions imposed on him by Mary's illness irksome enough. He was good to Mary, but the hearty fellow was ill adapted to self-sacrifice over a long period. Though he made a sincere effort to understand his wife, he sometimes felt it was impossible to close the gap between their differing natures.

Georgy was finally forbidden by both Dr. Patterson and Mahala to see his mother. The boy disobeyed and broke a window to get into his mother's room. The doctor then wrote to Abby, reporting that Georgy would not keep away and that this was proving injurious to Mary's health.

At this point, Abby had her hands full. She was working with her husband to build their business, brother Samuel was in difficulty, and the Tiltons were keeping his teen-age daughter; brother George was out of work and his young son had become lame.[7] As if this were not enough, Martha's youngest child, Mary Neal, became ill and passed away.

Martha wrote a brave letter to George, who was seeking work in the Midwest. After describing the situation, she explained:

Dr. Patterson is unable to pay me a dollar of interest this spring So I have to call on Mr. Tilton to pay all my debts and they are pretty heavy. What shall I do, foreclose at once? . . . Mary has been sick

"The house was near the main road beside a mountain stream."
Groton House, North Groton, New Hampshire,
maintained by the Longyear Foundation

several months and I expect they are brought to *absolute want!* He has done no work and takes care of her *alone.* . . . If I get my little property again in my possession I can tell better what I can do. But now I can only wait in a state of anxiety.

Despite her ill health and family obligations, Abby seems to have made the journey to North Groton to see for herself whether Dr. Patterson was correct in his assumption that the son's presence was injuring Mary's condition. Abby evidently came to the conclusion that Dr. Patterson was right. She perhaps felt that the situation had deteriorated to the point where there was no happy solution. Undoubtedly Abigail and Dr. Patterson and Mahala Sanborn Cheney held long discussions. Eventually, a plan reasonably satisfactory to all concerned, except of course to Mary, was arranged.

In the spring of 1856 the Cheneys were suddenly able to afford a move westward, something they had always wanted. They went to Minnesota, and Georgy, now nearly twelve, went with them. Mary had been with her son in North Groton only one short year. The relationship between mother and son, which had stretched and held by a thread through the most difficult circumstances, was finally broken.

Mahala later wrote a friend in Sanbornton that she regretted her adoption of the boy. As he grew older and was exposed to the free, rough ways of western frontier life, he became increasingly difficult to handle. Finally, when Georgy was seventeen, he ran away from home to join the army.

Despite his lack of education and his rough manner, there was something likable in the youngster as he grew to manhood. Though he did not meet her again for many years, Georgy retained an affection for his mother, and Mary cherished the memories of his childhood even in her last years.

Mary became gravely ill again, and Dr. Patterson found it necessary to nurse her. Martha was in despair over the doctor's unpaid debt. She had evidently given up her home, at least for the time being, and was keeping house for one of her relatives. Brother George was having difficulty finding work. Martha wrote despondently to Mathy in June, 1857:

I sometimes feel a fearful doom rests on our family — and yet tis so wicked to question the designs of Providence. . . . But why in every condition in life we must meet with disappointment and failure is a mystery. . . . Abby's visit to Mary has been constantly before my mind. . . . I hope it will not make dear Abby worse. . . . But Mary! poor child — alas, what words can express her condition. . . . O, may she yet feel to trust His goodness.

In the scrapbook that Mary kept at this time was a notation in her handwriting: "1857, May 7. Thursday. I slept very little last night in consequence of *memory* and wounded feelings."

She would not, however, give in to the despair that threatened to overwhelm her. She wrote in her journal of "the discipline, the darkness, and the trials of life." But her sister Martha's prayer that she might "yet feel to trust His goodness" was echoed in her heart. At this period Mary Baker Patterson made a solemn promise to God: if He restored her health, she would devote her remaining years to helping sick and suffering humanity.[8]

20   *"All things earthly must ultimately yield to the irony of fate, or else be merged into the one infinite Love."*
> *. . . Retrospection and Introspection*
> MARY BAKER EDDY

When Mary Baker Patterson was well enough, she attended the Congregational Church that stood on a hill overlooking the village of North Groton. Her questions about the dark trials of life were still unanswered, but she did not doubt God's righteousness nor the light to be found in her Bible. Sarah Turner, a niece of the Cheneys', commented as she looked back that "Mrs. Patterson was a person not easily

"... she attended the Congregational Church that stood on a hill overlooking the village of North Groton."
Maintained by the Longyear Foundation

forgotten." She remembered Mary as "a very spiritual woman," and recalled that "Mrs. Patterson frequently responded to the invitation to offer prayer, and her prayers were always uplifting and helpful." [1]

At times now, Mary seemed to draw on unexpected resources of spiritual courage and assurance. In her autobiography she would later write:

From my very childhood I was impelled, by a hunger and thirst after divine things, — a desire for something higher and better than matter; and apart from it, — to seek diligently for the knowledge of God as the one great and ever-present relief from human woe.

Her "hunger and thirst after divine things" was beginning to set her apart. She sensed that there was a careful search to be made and answers to be found. She knew that the things of Spirit must somehow be more real and substantial than the appearance of the world around her. When she was unable to go out of the house, she continued to read and ponder her Bible. Again and again, its assurances of help from God brought comfort. The Bible offered insights into an entire universe of God's goodness, far beyond what the eye could see. "Bring ye all the tithes into the storehouse," it was written in the book of Malachi, "... and prove me now herewith, saith the Lord of hosts, if I will not open you the windows of heaven, and pour you out a blessing, that there shall not be room enough to receive it."

One of Mary's visitors was an elderly gentleman known as Father Merrill. He was well over ninety years of age, but came every few weeks to read the Bible and pray with her. He firmly expected their prayers to have an effect, and on one occasion Mary did seem better as a result. But before long the symptoms returned, and Mary was again very ill.

Children would sometimes stop to talk with Mrs. Patterson on their way from picking berries. They called her "the good sick lady," and at home told of her comments to them about the Bible. Many of the townspeople, however, gossiped about Mary's invalidism and repeated tales of her "strange" ways.

Mary's companion and housekeeper at this time, Myra Wilson, recalled in later years that Mrs. Patterson read a great deal, that she "studied a large Doctor's book on homeopathy, and . . . some of the neighbors would come occasionally for medicine which she would give them." [2]

Homeopathy was a comparatively new system of medicine founded in Germany by Samuel Hahnemann. It had been introduced in New Hampshire early in the 1800's, and was rapidly gaining popularity. In contrast to allopathy, the more generally accepted system of medicine, it employed tiny, diluted doses of drugs in effecting its cures.

Not uncommonly, a sick person prepared his own medicine from a small kit of homeopathic drugs. Mary, in her long search for relief from suffering and her characteristic desire to see for herself, was studying the new system. Her experiments, however, were confirming her suspicion that it was actually the patient's faith in his medicine which was responsible for his recovery.

Once, while giving homeopathic pills to a neighbor, it occurred to her to try pellets which contained no medication.[3] The patient had been suffering from dropsy and improving with treatment, but Mary began to fear a reaction from prolonged use of the drug. Without telling the patient, she gave her unmedicated pellets. The woman continued to improve until she was well. Mary was beginning to feel sure that sickness was related in some way to a person's mental outlook. This piece of evidence furthered her growing conviction that all physical effects in the body actually had a mental cause.

On one occasion when making up Mary's bed, Myra knocked a bottle of homeopathic pills to the floor. "Mrs. Patterson noticed what I had done," the young woman recalled, "but she did not scold me, but told me not to mind as they were no good anyway."

Myra, a blind girl, was twenty years old. Mary had befriended the young woman and taken her into her home. Together they developed a workable arrangement for keeping house during those long days when Daniel Patterson was away. Myra was grateful to Mary throughout her life. While she recalled that her awkwardness would sometimes tax her invalid mistress' patience, she also remembered that Mrs. Patterson would immediately follow any sharp action or words with an impulsive hug and an apology.

Dr. Patterson had not been earning enough money for some time to support his home properly. He was not making the necessary payments on the house, and the Baker family's patience was becoming exhausted. Martha was in a difficult position, as she desperately needed the income.[4] In spite of her anguish about the situation, she was forced to foreclose.

It was then found that Dr. Patterson had other mortgages covering everything the couple owned, even Mary's gold watch chain and some of the furnishings that had come from her mother. Abby might have helped financially if the Tiltons had not had a large share of their money tied up in the reestablishment of their mill. The older sister undoubtedly realized now that any sum of money advanced to Dr. Patterson would only dwindle away and be impossible to recover.

Abby came with her carriage to move Mary from North Groton. Dr. Patterson was away. In a final note that must have made the experience seem like a nightmare, one of the Doctor's enemies gained entrance to the church on the hill and tolled the bell until the carriage was out of earshot. As Myra and the sisters drove slowly down the steep mountain road, Mary wept. Even though it was early spring and the road was muddy and rough, Myra finally left the carriage and walked behind. Mary's sobs were more than she could bear.

Years afterwards Mary included in her writings a passage which
could well have applied to this experience: "Remember, thou canst be

brought into no condition, be it ever so severe, where Love has not been before thee and where its tender lesson is not awaiting thee." [5] There must have seemed little tenderness in the episode at the time, but it was one of many trials which were, as Mary observed later, "graciously preparing" her.

Dr. Patterson made numerous fresh starts during the next ten years. Many earnest promises were made, but always they were broken. Daniel was kind and thoughtful with each fresh promise. He was struggling to live within the difficulties imposed by Mary's illness, and Mary for her part bore his erratic ways patiently. There were some times of genuine affection in spite of it all.

Dr. and Mrs. Patterson lived next in Rumney, where the dentist set up his office and began anew. Occasionally, Mary had visitors. Now, as through much of her life, she had a way of reassuring those who came to her in need. She looked forward especially to seeing children. One day a mother and her baby stopped by to see her. Mary noticed that the baby's eyes were seriously inflamed, and tenderly, with the great love she had for children, she took the baby in her arms. [6]

The mother was obviously anxious about the condition, but Mary lifted her thought to God, remembering Jesus' words: "Suffer the little children to come unto me, and forbid them not." Who, she asked herself, has forbidden this little one? Who is leading it into the way of blindness? Certainly it is not God! It seemed so clear and unquestionable. Gently, she returned the baby to its mother, saying a word or two about God's care for the child. After a moment, the mother glanced at the baby's eyes. Suddenly she exclaimed that they were perfectly clear and the baby could see.

It seemed natural — and wonderful. But it was only a momentary glance into a realm that Mary would later explore and chart more fully than anyone in the nineteen centuries since the time of Jesus and his earliest followers.

Two little girls who lived across the road from the Pattersons remembered that Mary was always writing. Grace and Nettie Hall called her "the pretty lady" and begged to be allowed to visit her. They recalled that their visit would be a reward for being especially good. On some occasions they were delighted to be left with Mrs. Patterson for half a day when their mother went into the village.[7]

Grace Hall told of how once when she had a tooth to be pulled, Mrs. Patterson took her on her lap and distracted her attention. The tooth was removed before the girl knew what had happened. The Hall girls remembered Dr. Patterson as a "fine-looking man," who was kind to his wife, carrying her about the house when she was too weak to walk. But another child later recalled the doctor as a man to fear. He apparently had more than one face, and varying moods.

Mary's couch was fitted with a headboard that could be raised or lowered by a cord. When she was lying down, she would ask the girls to take the string and pull her up. It was Grace Hall's recollection that the cord would sometimes slide from her hands, and Mrs. Patterson would fall back painfully. "Then," Grace remembered, "she would lie there and laugh at us." The girls would try again, this time much more carefully. In spite of pain, Mary was usually able to laugh. Her sense of humor never left her. It slipped into even her most serious writing.

Mary never stopped writing. She disciplined herself to write now, as she had to study when she was a schoolgirl. There was always a writing portfolio nearby, the Hall girls recalled, and the couch would be littered with sheets of Mary's notes and verses. If she was not writing, she was reading.

While Mary Patterson was spending much time in her quiet room in the small village of Rumney, the young American nation was by no means tranquil. Mary followed in the newspapers the election of Lincoln to the Presidency. She read of the heightened tension between

North and South on the issue of slavery and of the firing on Fort Sumter in the spring of 1861. Then the Union shuddered and broke in half. The great Civil War began.

Sometime later in the course of the war Mary received a letter which so excited her that she called in a neighbor to share her joy. Georgy had somehow managed to find her address.[8] The letter said that he was with the Northern Army's Eagle Regiment, looking forward to action in the South. It was the first direct news Mary had received of her son for over five years, and the fact that the letter was written on his own initiative made her happiness overflow.

News of the battles of Bull Run and Lincoln's call for volunteers now filled Dr. Patterson's thoughts. In the early spring of 1862 he found a mission as a civilian courier for the New Hampshire governor. Off the restless dentist went. But with typical carelessness, he strayed too near the enemy lines and was captured. His mission was ended practically before it had begun.

Mary did all she could to get help for her husband, writing to influential people she knew, and even to Franklin Pierce. Her health had taken a turn for the worse, but she contemplated making a trip to Washington to see what could be done. For the moment, however, no exchange of prisoners was being undertaken. There seemed no way to effect Dr. Patterson's release, in spite of the fact that he was a civilian.

For some months before Daniel Patterson left Rumney, reports of a man in the state of Maine who was accomplishing marvelous cures had reached New Hampshire. Phineas Quimby had been a clockmaker by trade, had learned about hypnotism, and given traveling exhibitions.[9] He had drawn certain conclusions about illness from his experience with hypnotism, gradually moving into the field of curing the sick through reasoning with them about the causes of their diseases. Before Dr. Patterson left, he had written Quimby regarding his wife's ill health, inquiring whether he planned to come to Concord, but Quimby did not wish to leave Portland at the time.

In desperation, Mary decided that she must find relief in one way or another, and through her sister Abby's assistance she was able to go to a water-cure sanitarium at Hill, New Hampshire. The so-called water cure was one of many health fads then popular in New England.

After several months, however, Mary had not improved, and at last she resolved that if Quimby could not come to her she would go to Portland to see him. She arrived exhausted, but before long felt better. Numerous tales of Quimby's marvelous cures were circulated among his patients, and his extreme confidence that everyone could be cured was reassuring.

Mary found him unlike anyone she had ever met before. He was kindly and idealistic in his way, earnestly desiring to help the sick. He spoke of the Bible and of Jesus' healings, though his methods were a mixture of bits and pieces of electromagnetic curist's methods and of what would today be recognized as a form of hypnotic suggestion.[10]

Quimby had immense conviction founded on his own experience of success in changing bodily symptoms through changing a person's mind. But, in a telling phrase, he said of himself in an advertising circular: "in his explanation lies the cure."

Mary talked with Phineas Quimby at length. He was deeply enmeshed in the details and the mechanics of his theory. But Mary immediately reached out for its broadest implications in regard to her Bible and her thought of God.

What she did not realize at the time was the powerful role which mental suggestion was playing in the healer's cures. Quimby did not consider himself a mesmerist, but the influence of one mind upon another which he had learned so well in his hypnotic exhibitions remained the major factor in his method.[11] The force of the clockmaker-hypnotist's personality was felt by most who met him.

Mary seemed greatly improved. Before long she characteristically put pen to paper and described her experience, praising Quimby highly. Her long letter was published in the *Portland Courier*.

Meanwhile, Daniel Patterson had escaped from the Confederate prison. By early November, he had made his way to Virginia and was given a letter of safe conduct from there to Washington. He reached New Hampshire in late November and was surprised to learn in Sanbornton that Mary had gone to Portland. In December he joined Mary. He lost little time in placing a notice in the *Portland Advertiser* which stated that "Dr. Daniel Patterson will give a lecture at Mechanics Hall . . . a condensed account of what he saw and heard among the rebels." Daniel's first lecture stirred little interest. In fact, it was frankly reported in the paper as a failure.

Not long after the Pattersons had returned to Sanbornton, Mary's old ailments reappeared. Without Quimby's compelling personality, the cure seemed to be fading. The action of one human mind upon another was proving a weak counterfeit of God's healing presence, of the spiritual things for which Mary Patterson thirsted.

21   *"When the door opened, I was waiting and watching . . . ."*
. . . Retrospection and Introspection
MARY BAKER EDDY

When Mary first returned to Sanbornton, apparently greatly improved, considerable interest was stirred in Quimby's power. Mary made an effort to hold on to the relief she had gained in talking with Quimby by writing what she remembered of their conversations. However, she included elements of her own reasoning and thoughts on the Bible. In a letter to an acquaintance living in Portland, she mentioned that she would "try to send my philosophy by Mrs. Tilton when she accompanies her son." [1]

Abby had been impressed by Mary's improvement, and took her son Albert to Portland to see whether Quimby might bring about a cure of the young man's recently acquired drinking habits. In Quimby's presence, Albert seemed to respond but, on returning home, quickly fell to drinking again. Abby concluded in the end that Mary's progress had not been due to Quimby. Mary, she declared, was healed by her own faith.[2]

During Mary's stay at the Bridge, the three Baker sisters visited friends, drove about the countryside, and worked on sewing projects to aid the Union soldiers. Mary particularly enjoyed seeing her nieces, Martha's daughter Ellen and Abigail's Evelyn.

Abigail and her husband had moved several years before and now owned the mill and house that once belonged to Augusta Holmes' family. The property was only a short distance downstream from the old Tilton place.

Mary could not help recalling the pleasant times they had all spent in this house. Here they had attended parties and talked for hours about teachers and studies and about what the future might hold. It was in this house that Mary had comforted Augusta when her father died, and where she said good-bye when Augusta married. How vividly it all came back! How close at hand, and yet how far out of reach! There had been births, marriages, and sorrow between that time and this; but it seemed almost possible to continue a conversation where it had broken off, to drop a note to Augusta once again, to expect to see all the usual friends one evening at a lively party.

There was no way to recapture these happy times nor the golden days of childhood at Bow by looking backward. Mary knew she must go forward. She was drawn on in her search for a clear understanding of the Bible and of Jesus' healing method.

But during the next several years there were many difficulties. Daniel Patterson was in and out of dental practice in various communities. He ranged widely in search of business, sometimes lectured on his experiences in the war, and seemed incapable of settling down. The couple established no permanent home, and there were long periods of separation.

Mary's health was still insecure. She sent letters to Quimby from time to time, asking for his further help. On several occasions she journeyed to Portland to renew her confidence in his theory of cure.

During these visits she was more persistent than other patients in questioning for herself and writing out her thoughts.[3] She made attempts to help others through Quimby's method, and once even gave a public lecture on the subject. But her observation in a letter to Phineas Quimby afterwards was significant. "This seems to me," she wrote, "a spiritual need of this people." From the first, she had seen Quimbyism through the lens of her lifelong study of the Bible and her pure yearning for divine things. A friend who knew her at this time in her life said that she seemed as "one fired with the prescience of a great mission."[4]

In July, 1864, Mary joined Dr. Patterson in Lynn, Massachusetts. There the couple had many acquaintances, for Mary made friends easily and the dentist was a likable fellow. She encouraged her husband to join a temperance lodge, the Good Templars, and she became active in the women's auxiliary.

Members of the lodge, pleased with her intelligence and gracious manner, elected Mrs. Patterson their presiding officer. A member of the lodge recalled that she "had a quiet way of commanding attention and in the delivery of an address was, in a strangely quiet way, impressive."[5] At the meetings, Mary sometimes read pieces she had written on the subject of temperance. Several of her articles and verses appeared in the *Lynn Weekly Reporter*. With the Civil War drawing to a close, her poetry and prose reflected the patriotism those times stirred in her thought.

In the fall of 1865 the Pattersons were living in Swampscott, Massachusetts. Here they had a second-floor apartment in a large house surrounded by gardens, including a brook and fountain. One member of the Lynn temperance lodge was George Newhall, a milkman. On his rounds he would often see Mrs. Patterson in the morning, sitting on the stone wall of the fountain, deep in thought, with a pad of paper in her lap. "She would write a little while," he recalled, "then gaze into the water a while, as if waiting for inspiration. While in those moods she wished no conversation with anybody." [6]

If she had once felt as though she were drifting without direction, now strong winds seemed to blow from several directions, and there was the need to set and hold a true course. Now she was being deeply stirred by thoughts about the possibility of healing others with no material aid, but with only the touch and the prayer of the Master. In her reading of the Bible she caught glimpses of uncharted deeps, and at times she was moved by an inner intuition of such uniqueness and hope it was difficult to share with others. It was not yet clear even to her.

While Mary Patterson made many friends, there were some who were not attracted to her because they said she spoke too often of religion. Possibly this hostility was based not on the frequency with which she mentioned religious subjects, but on the surprising force with which she did so. It was as though divine things were as tangible to her as everyday events. She was certain they could be grasped and understood. To some this certainty seemed vain and strange.

Mary's father passed on that fall. Dr. Patterson once again began leaving home. Then in January of the new year Phineas Quimby died. The slight anchor of assurance Mary had found in him was swept away.

During one of her husband's frequent absences in the winter of 1866, Mary went to a lodge meeting one Thursday night with several friends. It was exceptionally cold, as it can be in New England, with packed snow on the ground. The temperature hovered around zero, and the sidewalks were dangerously icy. As Mary walked along with the group, she suddenly slipped and fell.[7]

It was at once obvious to her friends that she was injured severely. They carried her, unconscious, into a nearby house and called the doctor, who confirmed their fears. Mrs. Patterson was suffering from grave head injuries, and there appeared to be a spinal dislocation.

In the morning, she was wrapped in fur robes and taken home in a sleigh. Her friends gathered at her apartment, for it seemed that she might not recover. The family living downstairs was greatly concerned. George Newhall, the milkman, was one of the first persons to come by on that bitterly cold day, and he was sent with a horse and sled two miles to call the minister. The Reverend Mr. Clark came as quickly as possible.

On Sunday morning, the minister stopped again to see Mrs. Patterson on the way to church. They prayed together, and she asked him to come by after the service. Mr. Clark replied by asking if she knew the critical nature of her injury and stated that she was sinking and might not survive through the day. Mary assured the minister that she did indeed realize all this. But, she told him, she had such faith in God that she felt He would raise her up.[8]

Since regaining consciousness she had refused to take any of the homeopathic medicine prescribed by the physician. Her faith was now in God alone.

When her good friends, the Browns, came by with their young daughter and promised to return in the evening, Mary told them, "When you come down the next time, I will be sitting up in the next room."[9]

"Mary, what on earth are you talking about!" Mrs. Brown exclaimed, concerned over whether Mrs. Patterson might not be delirious.

After her visitors left, Mary asked the friends who were staying with her to leave her alone. She wanted more than all else now to turn to the Bible, to seek what she believed so firmly must be there.

Again, Mary read of Jesus' healings. Then, as she read the ninth chapter of Matthew and the healing of the man who was paralyzed, a sense of peace came to her. Suddenly the full assurance of God's presence flooded her being with light. It was a revelation in which all the so-called facts of human experience melted away before one all-encompassing truth. "That short experience," Mary explained later, "included a glimpse of the great fact that I have since tried to make plain to others, namely, Life in and of Spirit; this Life being the sole reality of existence." [10]

Her thought soared fetterless and free, lifted upward as when a child she had answered, "Speak, Lord; for Thy servant heareth"; as when a child, in pure reliance on God, she was healed of fever; as when, with the unseeing baby in her arms, her consciousness was filled with the unquestioned assurance of God's great goodness, and the child saw!

Here was a sudden clear view of the reality of those divine things for which she had hungered and thirsted through the years. "When the door opened," she wrote later, "I was waiting and watching," and then she added, "Being was beautiful, its substance, cause, and currents were God and His idea." [11]

Mary realized that she was well. Her strength returned instantly. She was able to get up from bed and dress, and she went joyously to tell her friends.

The reaction of those friends was typical of what she was to encounter in the days that followed. At first they were pleased. But then disbelief crept in and, later, near hostility. They had not shared the experience themselves. Perhaps they felt it was too difficult to comprehend and easier, after all, to believe what they had always believed.

Mary could not explain in a way that satisfied them. She could only give the credit to God and God alone. While much in her earlier life had shown her how such healing might be possible, the experience itself was unlike all that had gone before. No words were adequate. As she had noted years before, human language was truly insufficient to tell of the things of Spirit.

143

For Mary Patterson the Bible from this time on was written in a new tongue. The Psalmist wrote: "In thy light shall we see light." For her the light had come; and now she would go forward in it.

22   *"The miracles recorded in the Bible, which had before seemed to me supernatural, grew divinely natural and apprehensible . . . ."*

. . . Retrospection and Introspection
MARY BAKER EDDY

There had been no medicine, no homeopathy, no vestige of mental suggestion in Mary Patterson's healing. There was only the inspiring sense of God as more real than all else. With this came healing. It was natural and immediate, as though lingering discordant notes had suddenly vanished in the resounding beauty of a true chord.[1]

It was unmistakably clear to her that God is the Principle of healing — the same God to whom she had turned as a child, the God of whom she had read all her life in the Bible. Mary had caught a glimpse of how much more God is than men commonly suppose as they go about their daily affairs. It was a breathtaking view, and it revolutionized her outlook upon the universe.

This new view changed Mary's concepts more radically than Copernicus' discovery of the planets orbiting around the sun changed his picture of the solar system. She saw that until there was some comprehension of the infinite, ever-present God, practically nothing was understood of life. Old concepts of God as manlike, a God who both loved and punished, disappeared. Perhaps because she already knew from bitter experience how little proof the five physical senses gave of God's all-powerful wisdom and goodness, she was ready to turn without reservation in a startling new direction.[2]

From this time on, any thought of matter as the real substance of the universe was to her hopelessly obsolete.[3] She had learned from her own

144

healing that the physical senses were unreliable. Her senses had told her only that she was injured and in pain. But upon opening her thought entirely to God, she had found completely different evidence — the wonder of God's loving presence and His care.

All her life she had questioned for herself. Now, in her forty-fifth year, she had no other goal in life than to discover and explore the full meaning of what she was learning. For three years after her healing, she devoted herself to discovering a positive rule which would bring healing to others. As when she was a child and had given away her coat, her first impulse was to share. She had not forgotten her solemn promise to God that if somehow her health could be restored she would give herself to helping humanity.

She thought of the Bible as her textbook, read little else for months, and wrote out lengthy commentaries on the Scriptures.[4] Gradually, she began to see clearly that the healing miracles recounted in the Bible were the natural outcome of divine law, unchanged in the nineteen centuries from Jesus' time to her own.[5] The words that she had read faithfully and obediently before now took on color and dimension. Vividly and accurately they described the experience of Christian healing just as she was learning it. Jesus had promised, "Ye shall know the truth, and the truth shall make you free." Her awe of the Master's life deepened with every step of her growing understanding of this truth which he had given mankind.[6]

At first it seemed that a lifetime — even centuries — of spiritual progress would be required before such a vast and exalted subject could be properly stated, much less demonstrated in practical terms.[7] It had been taken for granted that religion was something apart from the natural world and scientific truth. Yet she was certain that the divine laws upon which Jesus' healings were based constituted a more profound science than the world had ever known.

In her own words, her early "compositions were crude, — the first steps of a child in the newly discovered world of Spirit." [8] Immense work lay ahead. How was she, a lone woman, to do it? She was already forty-five years old, a time when some speak of slowing down. Mary Baker Patterson was speeding up. Increasingly, she turned to God for strength and wisdom, praying and listening earnestly for His direction.

Not long after her healing, Dr. Patterson again deserted her. This was to be the last time. She waited seven more years before obtaining a divorce from him. For twenty years she had been patient and forgiving. Dr. Patterson spent the last part of his life as an elderly recluse, regretting a wasted life. Mary again took the name of Glover, in memory of her first husband, George Washington Glover, and she was known once more as Mary Baker Glover.

Dr. Patterson had never been a good provider, but now there were times when Mary had barely enough money for her simple needs. Her mother's training now stood her in good stead. Abigail Baker had seen to it that her daughter was well versed in the frugal ways of New England farm life, and Mary never forgot these lessons. [9]

Thanks to her mother's instruction, and the time she had spent laying out patterns with her sisters, Mary Baker Glover was always dressed attractively. When she needed a new bonnet or gown, she could copy an expensive one that she had seen in a store. If she lacked the money to buy even the materials for making a new one, as sometimes happened, she could "make do" with careful mending. Or, with a deft touch, she could add a bright flower or a colorful ribbon. She had exquisite taste.

"She usually wore black," a young man said in describing her, "but occasionally violet or pale rose in some arrangement of her dress." [10] This was the recollection of George Clark, one of the young people Mary knew in Lynn and Swampscott. Wherever she lived, children and young people knew and loved Mrs. Glover. She had the complexion of a young girl and the vitality and buoyancy of youth. When she became deeply interested in a conversation, the color glowed in her cheeks and her eyes sparkled, even as in her childhood. Soft brown curls still framed her face. But it was primarily her outgoing love, her directness and spontaneity, and her delightful sense of humor that drew young people to her. As one young man put it: "You simply felt as if she was your best friend." [11]

George Clark remembered the colors Mary Glover wore because she had a "flower-like appearance." He never forgot her slender, graceful bearing as she sat at the table each night in his parents' boarding house.

Mary, who lived with the Clarks for a short time after Dr. Patterson deserted her, was seated at the head of the table. In his father's absence at this time, George sat at the foot and his mother in the middle. He remembered that

From this place at our table, [Mrs. Glover] easily dominated attention when she cared to talk, and she was always listened to with interest. Every one liked and admired her, though sometimes her statements would cause a protracted argument.

There were fourteen at the table, people from all walks of life. After dinner some would play whist, while others gathered around Mrs. Glover, and the discussions started at the table would continue.

Mary was slowly learning in these discussions how to convey to others something of what she was discovering. She felt compelled to share the thoughts which were so thoroughly absorbing her attention, and she gave her Bible notes and short manuscripts to her friends.

She found that the Phillipses, Quakers who were neighbors of the Clarks, enjoyed talking with her, and she spent much time in their household. It was as a result of her concern for Dorr Phillips, the son of the family, that Mary Glover first healed someone other than herself in accord with the divine laws she was discovering. [12] One day, when she stopped to visit, she found Dorr in great pain, with an infection called a felon on one of his fingers. "Dorr," she asked, "will you let me heal that felon?"

Dorr had heard Mary talking with his family about the Science that underlay the Bible healings and of how it could heal illness today. He was curious — and, more important, he was suffering. If Mrs. Glover thought she could ease the pain, he was willing that she should try almost anything. But first Mary warned him that while she was helping him he was not to try the usual remedies and that he must not look at the bandaged finger to see if it was healing. She had already learned through experience that to be healed one must turn wholly away from matter to God.

Dorr's married sister Susan lived only a short distance away. She was often at her parents' home, and had listened curiously to Mrs. Glover's talk of spiritual healing. That night when Dorr stopped at his sister's she inquired about his finger, knowing that it had been causing him much discomfort. "Nothing the matter with my finger — hasn't hurt all day," he said almost without thinking. Then he explained, "Mrs. Glover is 'treating' it."

"What is she doing to it? Let me look at it," Susan demanded.

"No, you'll spoil the cure. I promised not to look at it or think about it," he told her, "nor let any one else touch it or talk about it. And I won't."

The brother and sister looked at each other with half-smiles. They didn't know whether they believed or not.

"Tell me what she did," Susan begged.

"I don't know what she did — don't know anything about this business. But I'm going to play fair and keep my word," he told his sister. Then the young man forgot all about the finger — and later he found that the felon was gone.

Dorr's family was not ready to take the mere cure of a finger as anything approaching a miracle.

"No, it is not a miracle," Mrs. Glover tried to explain to them. "Nor would it be if it had been a broken wrist or a withered arm. It is natural, divinely natural."

She was sure that the healings which Jesus and his disciples brought about were not the result of some strange intervention by God but rather of the consistent action of divine law. She wrote later in her auto-biography: "I beheld with ineffable awe our great Master's purpose in not questioning those he healed as to their disease or its symptoms, and his marvellous skill in demanding neither obedience to hygienic laws, nor prescribing drugs to support the divine power which heals."

Through her prayers, Mrs. Glover next healed a young man who boarded with Susan and her husband. The young man had a fever, was delirious, and Susan was beside herself with worry.[13] He was the only son of wealthy parents who lived out of town. Susan was afraid to call the doctor until the parents arrived, but the young man was so sick that she also feared he might be dying. Mary went to his bedside and he immediately improved. Soon the fever was gone.

Several months later Mary had so interested one person in the prac-tical possibility of healing by relying totally on divine law that he requested she teach him this system. His name was Hiram Crafts. He was a heel finisher temporarily working in the Lynn shoe factories, and Mary had met Mr. and Mrs. Crafts while staying with the Clarks. In November of that year, the Crafts invited Mrs. Glover to stay with them on their return to their home in Avon, Massachusetts.

By the close of the year Mary had obtained the rational proof — the demonstration of this Christian Science — which she was pursuing.[14] In her earlier experiments with homeopathy she had learned that a per-son's thought produced effects on his body. But now it became increas-ingly apparent, as she reflected on her own experience in February and the other healings brought about that summer, that it was not her own mind that had affected the body in these healings. She realized she had been so conscious of God that all ordinary thoughts were absent; it was God or the divine intelligence — Mind — that was present.

In describing her discovery of Christian Science for a magazine article in 1904 she wrote: "I had found unmistakably an actual, unfailing causation, enshrined in the divine Principle and in the laws of man and the universe, which, never producing an opposite effect, demonstrated Christianity and proved itself Science, for it healed the sick and reformed the sinner on a demonstrable Principle and given rule." [15]

23

"Science and Health is the textbook of Christian Science."
. . . Retrospection and Introspection
MARY BAKER EDDY

In the spring of 1867, Mary Baker Glover was teaching her first student, Hiram Crafts, from her own manuscripts.[1] At last this naturally gifted teacher was teaching. Even though she had only one pupil, it gave her great joy. Her friends began to notice that the growing bundle of handwritten manuscripts was never far from her side. It seemed to be her most precious possession, as, indeed, it was.[2]

"These efforts," the author was to explain some years afterward, "show her comparative ignorance of the stupendous Life-problem up to that time, and the degrees by which she came at length to its solution." [3] While she never wished to have them published, she treasured these writings as mementos of her progress.

Although Mrs. Glover had one student, and some of her friends listened kindly to her explanations, there were many who began to shake their heads. They wondered at Mrs. Glover's "strange ideas." Those whom she healed said flatly more often than not that they could not understand. They were apt to forget the circumstances of the healing, along with their gratitude.

Though she had given herself wholly to her work, writing and studying for long, disciplined hours in her room, there were times when
memories of her family brought loneliness. Her thought would go back
over the years to the days of her childhood with "its starry hopes and its
waves of truth." [4] She thought of her mother's love, of her brother
Albert, of her first happy marriage, of her son. Shortly after she was
deserted by Dr. Patterson, she wrote her longings into a sad little poem
called "I'm Sitting Alone." [5] The poem recalled each loved one, and
ended:

I'm weeping alone that the vision is fled,
The leaves all faded, the fruitage shed,
And wishing this earth more gifts from above,
Our reason made right and hearts all love.

When her sister Abby offered Mary a home, there must have been
a great temptation to accept. The Tilton mill had brought Abby wealth,
and she told Mary that she would provide a home for her and "settle an
income upon you." She promised that they could all be together and
that Mary could still pursue her writing. But Abby set one condition. [6]

She had been hearing about Mary's strange ideas. There was only
one thing she asked. Mary was to give up those ideas which had lately
occupied her, attend the Tiltons' church, and abandon her theory of
divine healing.

Only one thing Abby asked! How little she knew *what* she asked!
With the perspective of later years, Mary understood and in no way
blamed her. She was to write: "My oldest sister dearly loved me, but I
wounded her pride when I adopted Christian Science, and to a Baker
that was a sorry offence." [7]

Mary Baker Glover was on a narrow bridge of decision. She could
go only forward or back. On one side, there was the family she loved,
and comfort — on the other, the lonely path. She did not hesitate, and
she replied to Abigail: "I must do the work that God has called me to do."

Abby did not believe her. She felt sure that her sister would one day yield and change her mind. But Mary did not. She only grew more certain of the vast meaning of her discovery, and she said later of this period: "The search was sweet, calm, and buoyant with hope, not selfish nor depressing." [8]

The author of her old school book had half hopefully guessed, "May there not be . . . Newtons in every science?" Mary Baker Glover knew now that there was scientific truth far deeper than that drawn from observation of physical facts. It was the truth of God's allness, and it changed forever the picture of a world made of matter.

In the history of Christianity there had been great reformers, preachers, and theologians. Mary was to take her place as Christian discoverer.[9] As surely as a Copernicus, Newton, Dalton, Fermi, or Einstein, she was willing to challenge ancient, accepted views to find truth. As she trusted and obeyed each of the insights which came to her, each led further into a universe of spiritual truths. Her search was quickened by the proof that Christian Science is able to help lift humanity out of suffering and sickness.

As she prayed and healed and wrote, the answers to questions of her earlier years began to appear. There could be no doubt now of God's will as entirely good for His children. He did not send sickness, but healed it.

For Mary Baker Glover the lives of the Master and the apostles had never before seemed so compelling. The Bible scenes glowed with realism, as though she, too, were present to hear the parables and the Master's teaching. As a humble follower of Christ Jesus, she prayed for still greater understanding of his words. She became certain that Christianity must again be seen as *truth,* as unparalleled *insight* into the nature of the universe and man.

Before long Mary again had an opportunity to test this Christian Science. In the summer of 1867, she received word that her niece Ellen

Pilsbury was dangerously ill. Quickly she decided to go to Sanbornton. For the first time in many years she was the one who could offer to help. She was sure that what she was learning of God could bring healing to Ellen.

Mary was able now to travel all the way to the Bridge by rail. The train took her along the Merrimack River through Bow, and she strained to catch a glimpse of the old farm as the cars sped her swiftly past. There was one stop at Bow Mills beyond the old Baker place, and another at Concord, where the train crossed the railroad bridge over the river and continued up the east side to Sanbornton.

On arrival, she found Martha's daughter so ill that no one entered her room except on tiptoe. Even a slight jar on the floor caused the patient great pain. The doctors whom the family had called had given her up, declaring that she was suffering from typhoid fever and enteritis. Ellen was unconscious and, everyone feared, at the point of death. Martha had already lost one child many years before, and there must have been great anxiety and fear in the household.

Mary asked to be left alone with Ellen. She stood quietly by the bedside. Her prayer was not one of imploring God to heal the sick girl. Instead, she turned her thought to God to know at that very moment nothing but His infinite goodness — goodness in which disease could no more exist than an area of darkness in a room full of sunlight.

The material evidence gave no indication of God's presence. But Mary had learned the falsity of such evidence. She was praying as Jesus prayed and taught his followers to do. She was conscious only of that truth which Jesus had promised would set free. She knew that God is good and that He is all, and that therefore evil is powerless and unreal.

In a few moments, the young woman recognized her aunt and spoke: "I'm glad to see you, Aunty." For about ten minutes more, Mary continued to pray. Then, quietly and firmly, she told Ellen to rise from her bed and walk. Ellen was not only able to do so but, at her aunt's request, walked back and forth across the room several times in perfect comfort. She was completely healed.[10]

This scene was in sharp contrast to Mary's sad visit with her brother George. He had been working in Wisconsin, but had been forced to come home. He was now very ill, blind, and deeply discouraged. But Mary was convinced that if her brother would only open his thought he would find healing. She poured out her heart in this final effort to help him. But George did not accept her views. Perhaps it seemed unlikely to him that the Mary he supposed he knew so well could have found a way to heal others through prayer. As Jesus had observed: "A prophet is not without honour, save . . . in his own house."

After her striking recovery, Ellen Pilsbury accompanied her Aunt Mary on her return to Avon, Massachusetts. At first, Ellen may have wanted to know more of this wonderful Science of healing. But when she realized how plainly her aunt lived, and how much study and self-sacrifice would be required of her if she was to learn about Christian Science, Ellen had no desire to stay.

After the niece returned home, misunderstanding flourished. Ellen carried sorry tales back home and turned completely against her aunt. Abby wrote in a letter to Mathy: "I have my private opinion that in the end no real good will result from all the stir she [Mary] has made about Ellen, but hope I am mistaken and great benefit will result from her efforts yet." The three sisters who had loved each other dearly were never close again.

Of all those in Mary's family circle, only one immediately acknowledged this healing work and expressed thanks, and this one was not her own kin. Mary's sister-in-law, Mathy Rand Baker, not only accepted the healing, but also wrote a letter to Mary verifying the facts.[11] Some years later she described the healing in detail for a visitor.

Mary's attitude toward her family is summarized best by a line from **154** one of her earlier letters to her brother George, who had misunderstandings at one time or another with most of his family. She wrote: "I cherish no unkindness in memory for you — I remember your kindnesses and your virtues — the rest is forgotten." [12]

As she left Sanbornton for the last time, Mary must have been tempted to feel that any link with the happiness of her childhood had been broken forever. But it was not to be so. As she continued along the road of discovery, she found that the golden days had not been lost. All that was good in the past now shone more brightly than before.

She turned with all her heart to the work before her. Soon she had another student, and then another. Gradually, her students began to heal others by following her example and her instruction. Her writing became increasingly important, for her manuscripts were vital to her teaching.

At first she wrote in the form of questions and answers. In 1870 she had copyrighted a manuscript called "The Science of Man"; and this, along with other notes and writings, was circulated among her students, though not published until 1876. [13] She explained in retrospect:

It was so new — the basis it laid down for physical and moral health was so hopelessly original, and men were so unfamiliar with the subject — that I did not venture upon its publication until later, having learned that the merits of Christian Science must be proven before a work on this subject could be profitably published. [14]

In the summer of 1870, Mrs. Glover held her first organized class, giving a course of twelve lessons. Still she found that healing was easier than conveying the full meaning of her discovery accurately to others. Once a prospective student was so startled at the suddenness of his first healing that he would have nothing more to do with this Science. On another occasion, Mary gave a lecture and healed one of the neighbors of her hostess of a serious illness. The notice for Mary's second lecture was torn down!

In January of 1872, a student who had not grasped the spirit as well as the letter of Christian Science ridiculed her views in a letter to a local newspaper. In reply came one of Mary's first public statements on Christian Science, published in the same newspaper.[15]

She now realized that if she wanted to make her discovery broadly available she needed more than manuscripts. She must write a book. In February of that year she began her work.[16] She continued to search the Scriptures and to write only as she felt clearly inspired and after she had waited selflessly for divine direction. Reason, revelation, and demonstration each played its part as the full significance of her discovery of Christian Science dawned on her thought. She had no sense of having personally invented a method or developed a new theory. She was instead discovering what was already *there* — like some lone voyager far in space coming suddenly upon a starry field stretching away infinitely in incredible richness and beauty.

She would later write of angels as "God's thoughts passing to man; spiritual intuitions, pure and perfect. . . ." [17] It was well that Mary Baker Glover had her angels. She was borne on by these pure, joyous intuitions through the trials and loneliness that engulfed her in these years. Through 1872, 1873, 1874, she found lodging as best she could, being forced to move many times. Frequently, people said that her ideas were absurd and they wanted nothing to do with her.[18] Once she had been turned out at night during a rainstorm, with no place to go. At one point, her only possession was the rocking chair in which she sat and wrote. Her desk was a piece of cardboard from the back of an old book.[19]

The first chapter of her book was to be called "Natural Science." [20] Here she carefully set forth definitions of those terms she would use in helping others comprehend her discovery. She was well aware of the difficulty of having to employ words to describe the spiritual universe which she was exploring. It was like trying to capture the flowing music of a grand symphony in sentences — only infinitely more demanding.

She saw plainly the need for a precise use of language. Over the years she was to make changes in the terms she had originally used, in order to make her meaning unmistakably clear. She spoke of God, divine Spirit, as *immortal Mind*. The mind which seemed to reside in the body she called *mortal mind*. All that was eternally true was learned from *Mind*. The physical senses she called *error* and *shadow*. In the chapter called ''The Great Discovery,'' in her autobiography, she was to explain:

I knew the human conception of God to be that He was a physically personal being, like unto man; and that the five physical senses are so many witnesses to the physical personality of mind and the real existence of matter; but I learned that these material senses testify falsely, that matter neither sees, hears, nor feels Spirit, and is therefore inadequate to form any proper conception of the infinite Mind.

Often people made fun of Mary Glover's Science. At times they were openly hostile and rude. However, when alone with her writing, she was full of joy. A book had been in her thoughts since childhood. Now she was writing one, but it was different from anything she could ever have hoped or imagined. Nothing could wholly discourage her now. She pressed on, teaching and healing and, above all, writing. Sometimes as she wrote, the words would come so fast to her receptive thought that she let the papers fall to the floor, gathering them up at the end of the day.

Young people caught the intensity and the scope of her vision more readily than those who were older. One of the boys who knew her in this period wrote:

I was sixteen years old when Mrs. Eddy lived in Stoughton [Avon], and I remember her very well. I recall that as often as two or three nights out of every week for over two years, I used to visit Mrs. Eddy with other young folks of the town. . . . We were in the habit of visiting her to listen to her talks, for even then she was regarded by those who knew her as a wonderful woman. . . . Some of the

most pleasant recollections of my youthful days center in that little
room at the Wentworths' [where Mrs. Glover was staying].[21]

She had carefully saved the money she received from teaching.
She had not had her own home for many years, and she longed for a
place of her own, where she could find peace in which to study and
write whenever she felt impelled. At this time she had no steady
income, but still she was determined to save so that she could buy
her own home.

During most of these years she was living in the area of Lynn,
Massachusetts, near the ocean. When she had written all she could for
the day, she would often walk down to the sea. Her favorite spot was
at the headland where great red rocks jut out from the shore. She
would make her way over the rocks to the place where they ended
the curve of the sandy beach and pointed out to sea. She loved
Red Rock as she had loved the granite rocks at Bow. Here there were
no doubting people — only wind and sky and the sound of the sea.[22]
The beauty of nature sustained and comforted her.

By September of 1874, Mary felt she had finished her work.[23]
With the manuscript in hand, she was able to find a printer in Boston
who was willing to undertake publication. He began to set the type.
Then, unaccountably, he stopped his work. No message Mrs. Glover
sent him moved him to go ahead with the book. By March, 1875,
with the added sense of responsibility for her students, she was
growing concerned. She prayed earnestly to find the answer to why
the book was delayed.[24]

At the time, she was living in a house on Broad Street in Lynn.
One day, as she sat in her upstairs room looking out the window at the
bleak March sky and the stark branches of the treetops, she heard the
people in the room below talking noisily. It might well be that they
were joking about Christian Science as they often did. How much

longer, she wondered, must things continue this way? Again, she prayed that she might find her own quiet home.

Across the street, there was a small house. Now, as she looked at it more closely, she noticed a sign stating that the house was for sale. She had managed to save enough for an initial payment, and with great happiness, she purchased the property. At last she was home.

When Mary Baker Glover moved into her house, there was little money left out of her small reserve, so she rented most of the home to others. However, she kept the front parlor for teaching her students and the small attic room on the third floor for herself. The room was tiny, with a low, sloping ceiling, but it was peaceful and all her own. Its only light came from the skylight, a small window in the side of the roof. Looking upward, Mary could see only sky and the clouds and stars.

Still her book had not gone forward. Then, as she prayed to see why the work was not completed, she realized that her own work was not finished. She saw clearly the need to point out the dangerous counterfeit of spiritual healing — the influencing of one person by another through suggestion and willpower. This hypnotic or mesmeric influence, as it was then termed, was the exact opposite of healing through having that mind "which was also in Christ Jesus."

It seemed a painful task, but obediently she began to write in the peace of the attic room. Her rocking chair was placed under the skylight window. Like the child Mary, in the little rocking chair at Bow, she was still willing to be alone, still quietly studying the Scriptures. Gradually, she realized why the book had not been printed. She inserted a section exposing the evil dangers of hypnotic influence, and the printing of the book then went forward without delay.

Mary had waited patiently for six weeks for God to show her what the name of the book should be.[25] Then while lying awake one night, the title *Science and Health* came gently to her thought. She arose at once and wrote it down. *Science and Health with Key to the Scriptures* she later gave as the book's full title. It was the key she had found to the Bible. It answered the questions of her childhood and explained how Jesus healed.

In the small room so close to the stars, Mary Baker Glover finished her book. It is the textbook of Christian Science, and it begins:

"To those leaning on the sustaining infinite, to-day is big with blessings." [26]

"In the small room so close to the stars, Mary Baker Glover finished her book."
Lynn Historical House, Lynn, Massachusetts, maintained by the Christian Science Church

Epilogue

What appears to be the end of the story is, in truth, but another beginning. In the years from that memorable day in the small attic room in Lynn, Massachusetts, when she finished her book, to the June day in 1903 when she stepped out upon her balcony to speak to the crowds gathered below, Mary Baker Eddy had worked and prayed more tirelessly than ever before.

Her book went through many revisions, as she poured into it her continuing experience in teaching and healing. Her purpose was always to help the reader see clearly what she herself had seen. She wrote: "I have revised SCIENCE AND HEALTH only to give a clearer and fuller expression of its original meaning." [1] Many who gathered below her balcony on that June day could say with all their hearts not only that the meaning of the book was clear, but that it was truth which had entered their lives as irresistibly as the coming of daylight. It had brought healing and a new view of the world.

Some months after the publication of *Science and Health,* a new student came to Mrs. Glover for healing. His health improved almost immediately, and he joined the small group which was dedicating itself to making Christian Science more widely known. His name was Asa Gilbert Eddy. He proved quick to understand and wholly devoted to the new work. In January of 1877, Mary Glover and Gilbert Eddy were married. Afterwards they were given a quiet party by the little family of students of Christian Science. For them, as much as for Mary, this occasion seemed to mark a strengthening of their cause.

Gilbert Eddy entered the public practice of Christian Science healing and conducted an early Christian Science Sunday School. He taught a special Bible class, helped with the teaching of Christian Science, and, Mrs. Eddy noted, "lectured so ably on Scriptural topics that clergymen of other denominations listened to him with deep interest." [2] Five years were shared together before her husband's passing, but Mrs. Eddy had found in him the reliable strength and companionship so much needed at that time in her life. She kept the name of Eddy, and so the Discoverer and Founder of Christian Science became known to the world as Mary Baker Eddy.

In the spring of 1879, twelve students of Christian Science voted "To organize a church designed to commemorate the word and works of our Master, which should reinstate primitive Christianity and its lost element of healing." [3] It was a startling statement. In a few words it caught the full force of what those studying with Mrs. Eddy were learning. They had seen pain and illness recede before the fearless, quiet assurance of a universe filled with the goodness of God.

A visitor to one of their meetings at this period spoke of "the little circle of followers which meets for fellowship at her [Mrs. Eddy's] house fortnightly." [4] He observed, "They take the name of Christian Scientists and find in the Christian Records the foundation of their faith." Later he commented, "I find her followers thoughtful and devout, without cant or egotism, students of life rather than of books, and a promising company."

If they seemed promising it was not for the usual reasons. Of education, wealth, or social background, they had little. It was the quality of their inner conviction — what they knew they had seen — that set them apart.

As a result of her teaching, writing, healing, and preaching, Mary Baker Eddy saw the number of those who called themselves Christian Scientists rapidly increase. She was not only the Discoverer of Christian Science but also the Founder and Leader of the church organization which would make it known to mankind for the years to come.

She wrote other books explaining her work. She founded and edited *The Christian Science Journal* and established the *Christian Science Sentinel,* to which students of Christian Science could contribute their own articles and in which they could share accounts of healing. In addition, she taught classes in Christian Science as far away from New England as Chicago and Washington, D.C. Once she addressed an audience of four thousand in the vast Central Music Hall in Chicago and, another time, one of over a thousand at Steinway Hall in New York City.

Still there were hard battles to be fought. Some religious leaders of the time attempted to ridicule Christian Science, saying that it could heal only imaginary diseases or that Christian Science was unchristian or that it denied all the laws of common sense. Newspapers and magazines frequently published bizarre distortions of Mrs. Eddy's life in order to stir curiosity and to attract a wider readership. But gradually there were some who, although they were not Christian Scientists, rose to defend the right of Christian Scientists to practice their religion without persecution. Many who disliked Mrs. Eddy or Christian Science found, when they actually investigated, that Christian Science was not at all what they had supposed it to be.

As churches were built throughout the world, Mrs. Eddy faced the problem of a great variety of personal views being substituted for the spiritual discovery which she had named Christian Science. After praying to be guided, she took the radical step of discontinuing all personal preaching in these churches. Instead there would be readings from the Bible and from the Christian Science textbook, *Science and Health with Key to the Scriptures.* The page and line numbers of these passages would be printed ahead of time, so that church members could study them carefully before hearing them read at the Sunday service. Thus the Lesson-Sermon would be the only "preacher," and the subject would be the same on any given Sunday in Christian Science churches around the world.

The subjects of the Lesson-Sermon — twenty-six in all — would be repeated twice a year, but the passages selected from the Bible and *Science and Health* would always be fresh. Among the twenty-six subjects chosen by Mrs. Eddy were Spirit, Love, Christ Jesus, Doctrine of Atonement, Everlasting Punishment, Matter, Mind, and Is the Universe, Including Man, Evolved by Atomic Force? [5]

It was obvious that the Discoverer of Christian Science was looking both backward to her own childhood and forward to the new century.[6] She was making certain that those questions that had troubled her own youth would be dealt with for future generations through these Bible Lessons. But she predicted, "The twentieth century in the ebb and flow of thought will challenge the thinkers, speakers, and workers to do their best." [7]

Mary Baker Eddy never believed that religion should narrow its attention to a few dusty topics that might safely be called religious. She had found men's concept of God too limited, and knew that in proportion as their idea of God expanded, all of life took on new meaning. "No form nor physical combination is adequate to represent infinite Love," she wrote. "A finite and material sense of God leads to formalism and narrowness; it chills the spirit of Christianity." [8]

Her range of interests was extensive. It had not been restricted, but broadened and deepened by her discovery. Her capacity to discern the needs and yearnings of others was heightened. She read widely and kept herself well informed of world events, of discoveries in the natural sciences, of religious trends.[9] Perhaps no single event of her career gave such a sharp indication of her view of religion's central position in the midst of life as the establishing of a great international daily newspaper to be published by the church she had founded. Her launching of *The Christian Science Monitor* near the close of her life showed her keen concern for the world and its people.

In 1894, the first large Christian Science Church building was constructed, in Boston, Massachusetts. As the home church for Christian Scientists all over the world, it is known as the Original Mother Church edifice. Soon Christian Science churches, known as branch churches, were established in England, Germany, and other countries. *The Manual of The Mother Church, The First Church of Christ, Scientist, in Boston, Massachusetts,* written by Mrs. Eddy, formed the basis for governing the fast-growing denomination.

In only a few years, a much larger church building was required in Boston for the increasing numbers of Christian Scientists who wished to attend services. The huge domed Extension of The Mother Church, one of the largest church structures in the United States, was completed in 1906.

Mary Baker Eddy never visited the beautiful new church, though great must have been her desire to see it. She had found that people tended to pay too much attention to her and not enough to the truths she wished them to grasp. One day, however, when she was living in nearby Chestnut Hill, she decided that she would go after all to visit the imposing structure. She started to leave her home, but got only as far as the front door, then turned back. Returning her shawl to Laura Sargent, one of her devoted students, Mrs. Eddy said, "That was Mary wanting to go." Always she endeavored to keep it God's way — not Mary's.[10]

Although her only child, George Glover, remained in the West, Mary did have a chance to see him on several occasions. Once he surprised her with a visit, and Mary recognized him immediately, though he had grown to manhood during the years they were apart. At another time George was estranged from his mother through misleading information that was given him.[11] But he had acted from his mistaken sense of duty, not from his lack of love.

George owned mines and lived for many years in Lead, South Dakota, in a handsome home for which his mother had furnished the money. Mrs. Eddy lived to enjoy her grandchildren, who visited her a number of times. She treasured the gifts the family gave her, one of which was a pin fashioned like a gold miner's pan, with crossed shovel and pick. Mrs. Eddy healed her granddaughter and namesake,

Mary, of crossed eyes.[12] A great-grandson served in the Navy during World War II, and was a Christian Science Volunteer Wartime Worker.[13]

Mrs. Eddy's hair turned snow white over the years, but she retained a youthful appearance and buoyancy of thought and action. It was a continuing surprise to those who met her in later years. At times, when she was going through some particularly trying experience, the struggle would show in her face. There were other times when the color of her eyes would deepen and flash with anger at some false accusation or injustice. But the luminous depth of her eyes and the smile that some say has never been truly captured in a portrait would always return.[14]

After the initial founding of her church in Boston, Mrs. Eddy lived for some years in Concord, New Hampshire, in a home she named Pleasant View. She would have liked to live in Bow, on the site of the old home, but the location was inconvenient both for visitors and the members of her large household. She chose instead a house that overlooked the hills of Bow.[15] Often she would take visitors to her study window and point out to them the location of the old Baker farm.

New Hampshire *was* proud of its daughter. During her lifetime, a book entitled *New Hampshire Women* included a portrait and major tribute to Mary Baker Eddy. The city of Concord had shown its regard for this well-known citizen on numerous occasions. To the mayor and city council of Concord, Mrs. Eddy once wrote:

My home influence, early education, and church experience, have unquestionably ripened into the fruits of my present religious experience, and for this I prize them. May I honor this origin and deserve the continued friendship and esteem of the people in my native State.[16]

In deference to Mrs. Eddy, Concord made special plans to welcome those Christian Scientists who were to come at their Leader's invitation on that memorable day of June 29, 1903. In the beginning the day was rather cool, with some threat of rain, but no one in town had time to worry over the possibility. Everyone was much too busy making ready for the great throng expected at Pleasant View.[17]

Many of Mrs. Eddy's fellow townspeople joined the crowd of Christian Scientists, as special trains let them off at the depot and they drove or walked out Pleasant Street to Mrs. Eddy's home. One lady in a big straw hat decorated with red roses escorted two small boys by the hand. "We must hear Mrs. Eddy," she told them, "because even though we do not agree on religion, she is a great woman, and we should be proud to have her live in our city." [18]

Two girls in a pony cart made their way along the street, entranced at the sight of dignified Christian Science gentlemen in top hats sitting on the curb eating sandwiches out of a paper bag.[19]

In a marvel of order, thousands of members of the Christian Science Church had been transported from Boston to Concord by the railroad on twenty-four hours' notice. Concord took care of the visitors after they arrived with equal efficiency.[20]

One of the passengers on one of the special trains was twelve-year-old Alice Noble. She wrote in her diary that she had wanted to go "like everything," but could not "afford the $1.60." [21] However, she had found a way to obtain the money and was at Pleasant View with her Aunt Eva. They were two hours on the train, but had taken their lunch.

When we got there, there was an awful crowd; but you didn't mind. No one did, not even when it rained did anyone express regret. We had to wait an hour. Then Mrs. Eddy (. . . she lives in a lovely house, light green) came out on the second balcony and made a speech. Mrs. Eddy is lovely. She has the . . . loveliest, purest face, and was dressed in a purple velvet and ermine cape. I always imagined that she was quite large but she was small. She kissed her hands and waved to us. We all sang *Shepherd Show Me How to Go* and *Saw Ye My Saviour* [Mrs. Eddy's poems which had been set to music]. After it was all over it was as still, no one clapped or made a sound. The men stood with heads uncovered and some of the ladies waved their handkerchiefs. Mrs. Eddy then went out to drive and we saw her again. She smiled so sweetly. Wouldn't it be wonderful not to have to share or divide the smile between all, but to have one all to yourself. I think it would make a change in your whole life.

The experience may indeed have changed Alice's whole life. In *Science and Health with Key to the Scriptures* Mrs. Eddy had written: "While age is halting between two opinions or battling with false beliefs, youth makes easy and rapid strides towards Truth." [22]

Alice went on to study the textbook of Christian Science earnestly. She knew and loved Mary Baker Eddy better with each passing year, for, as the Discoverer and Founder of Christian Science had said, "They who know (understand) my book, know me." [23]

Notes

Notes: Prologue

1. The scene was described in Boston newspapers, including the *Boston Herald* of June 30, 1903, and is reported in the *Christian Science Sentinel,* Vol. V, July 4, 1903, p. 696.

A photograph of the scene at Pleasant View hangs in the Board Room of the First Church of Christ, Scientist, in Concord, New Hampshire. The well-known balcony portrait of Mrs. Eddy was enlarged from a similar photograph.

2. Archives of The Mother Church, The First Church of Christ, Scientist, in Boston, Massachusetts (hereafter identified as Archives).

Notes: Chapter One

1. The diary of Joshua Lane (New Hampshire Historical Society) and the *New Hampshire State Register* give a good day-by-day description of that year's weather. The diary includes a wealth of information about farming. Erwin D. Canham, who spent his boyhood on a Maine farm, supplied the author with much useful information about haying and cider making.

2. Reconstruction of the appearance of the Baker farm is based on a variety of source material. The monograph published in 1914 by the Woodbury E. Hunt Company of Concord, New Hampshire, *The Birthplace of Mary Baker Eddy, Bow, New Hampshire,* was helpful. It describes in detail the research that took place before Edward L. Henry painted his well-known picture of the old Baker farmhouse.

Rufus H. Baker did an engraving of the old homestead and sent it to Mrs. Eddy for approval. She replied in part (Archives): "Accept my thanks for the well executed engraving of the Baker homestead. Around the memory thereof clusters the golden days of my childhood. . . ."

The Rufus Baker engraving was useful, as were photographs at Longyear Foundation,

Brookline, Massachusetts. These photographs show the front half of the house, after the saltbox portion had been ripped away.

Joseph Baker had divided his farm between three sons, James, Philip, and Mark. The last two sold their farms in 1835. Eventually, James's son Aaron bought back most of the land. By then, however, the Mark Baker homestead was no longer needed as a dwelling. Aaron's son, John Baker, moved the remnant of the house across what is now the turnpike and used it for storage. Its history ended when it was destroyed by fire.

The land on which this remnant of the old house stood, land owned by the Bakers since the time of Hannah Lovewell Baker, is still in the possession of a later John Baker, a descendant of Hannah and Joseph. The modern New Hampshire turnpike now cuts through the old farm, directly behind the site of Mark Baker's home, which is maintained by the Christian Science Church as an historical landmark.

Inspection of sites, including the overgrown and forgotten cellar hole of the home that belonged to James, Aaron, and John Baker, as well as interviews with old-timers in Bow, helped piece out details of the setting. Abstracts of deeds, researched as a hobby over a period of many years by the late Willoughby Colby of Concord and Bow, were especially valuable in reconstructing Bow as it was in the 1820's and 30's. Richard Hansen, a selectman, and Mrs. George Morrill and her late husband, who acted as caretaker of the old Baker home site for a number of years, also assisted.

3. Sarah (Sally) Knox Gault has sometimes been confused with another Sarah "Gault." This mistake comes from an error in the manuscript of the "History of Bow," by Harrison Colby, Vol. II, New Hampshire Historical Society. The second Sarah was not a Gault, but a Gile, and resided in Nottingham, not Bow, New Hampshire. She was a relative of the Samuel Gault family, also neighbors of the

Bakers. "Nottingham Vital Records, 1734-1877," p. 39 (N.H.H.S.). "Vital Records of Bow, New Hampshire, 1710-1890," Priscilla Hammond (N.H.H.S.).

4. Mrs. Eva Alexander, a native of Bow who lives on the site of the Andrew Gault home, states that the well-worn path was used by her grandchildren until the new turnpike cut through the countryside. Mrs. Eddy refers to this path in material in the Archives of The Mother Church.

Letters in the possession of Longyear Foundation and the Archives, from the grandchildren of Sarah and Andrew Gault, verify the close relationship between Sally and Abigail Baker, as well as the friendship between the families. Mrs. Eddy told the story of her mother's experience as related here to her students, including Clara Shannon and Adam Dickey, who describe it in their memoirs (Archives).

Notes: Chapter Two

1. According to the Bow town book, "Early Records, Births, Deaths, Marriages, 1767-1820" — otherwise known as "The Upside Down Book," because it can be read from either end when turned upside down — Maryann Baker gave birth to eight boys and two girls between the years 1763 and 1785. One son died at the age of four in 1776.

2. Mark Baker's account book at Longyear. *Diary of An Early American Boy,* Eric Sloan (1962).

3. *New Hampshire Patriot and State Gazette,* May 19, 1823.

4. According to Reverend Nathaniel Bouton's *History of Concord* (1856), it cost one dollar to travel by stagecoach to Boston, a distance of sixty miles by way of the old turnpike. This was a cut in price, occasioned by competing stage lines.

The ledges referred to as "the playground" were uncovered by the author's Cub Scout Den in an "archeological" expedition.

Early town histories, in particular those of Pembroke, Bow, Concord, and Sanbornton, have been most helpful in the gathering of details. This material was compiled many years ago, and in a number of cases the author found it more accurate than recently written history.

5. Bouton's *History of Concord,* p. 644. *The Ancestry of Mary Baker Eddy* (1915), J. Gardner Bartlett, pp. 108, 109. *Ambrose Genealogy,* John Lee Ambrose, about 1909 (N.H.H.S.).

6. Mary once wrote to George (Thanksgiving, 1850, Longyear) referring to a misunderstanding: ". . . that I have erred I penitently acknowledge. My temper is hasty but not sullen . . . I thought 'twas too cruel and *unmerited* for me to bear and reflected not on the consequences." See also, Mary Baker Eddy, *The First Church of Christ, Scientist, and Miscellany,* 310:26.

7. Bow tax records. These records tell precisely how many farm animals Mark Baker owned during each year of his residence in Bow.

8. John Baker's will, 1665, at Longyear Foundation.

Notes: Chapter Three

1. Several spellings have been found for "Maryann" Baker, but this was the form she used in signing her name in the record book for the Union Church in Bow, and in certain other papers.

2. *Mary Baker Eddy, Discoverer and Founder of Christian Science: Her Life and Ancestry* (1930), National Americana Society, Inc., New York; and Bartlett's *Genealogy.*

3. The *History of Pembroke* was written by

the Reverend N. F. Carter in 1895. The Baker and Ambrose families are mentioned frequently, and the genealogical tables have been used many times by Mrs. Eddy's biographers. Some errors in the genealogical tables of both families are reflected in biographies of Mrs. Eddy.

4. Records for the town of Bow have been well preserved and are kept in the town hall. They present an accurate picture of Joseph and Mark Baker's status in the town. A stack of well-worn record books was examined carefully over a two-year period with the assistance of the late Annie Colby Foote, town clerk for over forty years.

5. Since Bow was located on the turnpike, the direct route to Boston, and the Baker home overlooked the pike, the family may well have been roused by riders. The town record book lists the battles as given here, noting amounts of money paid to those men who served in each battle. Bow citizens, according to the record, "went to Lexington upon the alarm."

Notes: Chapter Four

1. Several sources were used in the historical reconstruction of the interior of the Baker home. Most interesting is the Solomon Richardson house in Old Sturbridge Village, Massachusetts. This reconstructed village (open to the public as a living museum) is of the same period as that covered in the early chapters of this book (1790-1840) and gives an unexcelled picture of this era.

The Richardson house, as nearly as can be ascertained from the material at hand, is a duplicate of the old Baker home in most respects. It is of saltbox construction, like the Baker home, and has a similar window and room arrangement.

The historic Hartwell Farm in Lexington, Massachusetts (open to the public as a restau-

rant), also has the same general room arrangement and appearance of the Baker farmhouse, although it is not a saltbox.

Two photographs of the interior of the Baker house may be seen at Longyear, although these show the rooms as they were at least 60 years after the Bakers left.

The research of Edward L. Henry for his painting, and the publication of the Society for the Preservation of New England Antiquities, *Old Time New England,* Vol. XLVIII, Number 171, "Notes on Furnishing a Small New England Farmhouse," added authentic detail.

2. The clock was made by Levi and Abel Hutchins of Concord. It is on exhibit at the Mary Baker Eddy historical house at Lynn, Massachusetts.

3. Archives.

4. The inventory of the will of grandfather Joseph Baker was found on record at Exeter, New Hampshire. As was customary, it lists all of his possessions at the time of his passing, giving a good idea of what was found in the home inherited by his son Mark. Included were cooking utensils and houseware, light stands, a sleigh and harness, looking glasses, a canoe, books, farm implements and animals. There was also furniture — in particular, a desk, later to be used and cherished by Mark. According to Mark Baker's will (Longyear), this desk was left to his son George, along with the grandfather clock and other personal possessions.

5. Two pieces of needlepoint done by Mary Baker were kept in the Baker family and are still in existence, one a picture of a Madonna and child (Longyear), the other an intricate floral pattern (Lynn historical house).

6. Mark Baker's desk and Abigail's rocking chair are on exhibit at the Longyear Baker Room, along with other personal belongings of the family.

7. *New Hampshire State Registers,* 1817-1835.

8. The produce of the farm was listed in a legal agreement between Mark and Aaron Baker, January 7, 1829 (Longyear).

9. Letter of Martha to George, January 20, 1836.

The Longyear collection of Baker family letters written during the period 1835 to 1856 has been of value in forming an understanding of the character of Mark and Abigail Baker and their children. These letters are referred to extensively in the following chapters. Unless otherwise noted, all family letters are from the Longyear Foundation, Brookline, Massachusetts. The author is very grateful for permission to use and to quote from this invaluable collection.

10. Lyford's *History of Concord* (1903), pp. 1243, 1248. *History of the Schools of Concord. Iron Works Anecdotes* (School District #18, Concord), George Abbot, 1886 (N.H.H.S.).

11. "Brief History of the Congregational Church in Pembroke," Rev. Isaac Willey (1876). "Discourse at the Funeral of Rev. Abraham Burnham," Rev. Mr. Noyes (1852). Mr. Burnham is mentioned prominently in the church records of the surrounding towns where he often preached, and in town histories, especially those of Bow and Concord.

12. George copied some of Mary's poems into his "Journal" (Longyear). The brother and sister exchanged poems on at least two occasions: Mary's departure from home at the time of her marriage and on the death of the mother. Martha refers in one letter (August 6, 1837) to George's writing, but the reference seems more in a teasing vein than complimentary. George wrote at least one romantic piece of fiction for the *Belknap Gazette,* according to his journal.

13. Only a few of the old school record books remain for the town of Bow. Fortunately, the record book for School #3, 1807-1862, has survived and was found among the town books. It not only shows that Mark Baker took an active part in his school district from the time he was married, but also dispels the confusion that has arisen over the location of the school attended by Mary Baker. There were only seven school districts at this time.

Because the 1858 map of Bow shows the location of another school, District #8, up the hill from the Baker home, it has been thought by some that this was the school attended by the Baker children. According to the record book, the Bakers were always in District #3, and the location of the school is given specifically as at the crotch of the road "between the turnpike and the old county road." Of particular interest was the discovery that Albert Baker taught in this school. (See discussion in Chapter 8, p. 50, of this book.) The first printed report of the Superintending School Committee for the town of Bow, in 1848, gave additional background.

14. Mrs. Eddy spoke several times of this incident to her students. It is mentioned in the memoirs of Clara M. Shannon and in a letter in the Archives of The Mother Church. There is another related incident, concerning Mary at four or five years. In this she plays a game with her friends at recess and gives the same answer to the inquiry. It seems quite possible that both stories are accurate and reflect an early desire to write a book.

Notes: Chapter Five

1. Mrs. Baker to Mary, May 6, 1844.

2. Russel B. Nye, *The Cultural Life of the New Nation, 1776-1830* (1960), p. 142.

3. Reminiscences by Mary Angeline Walkley Beach (1824-1897) in the article "Notes on Furnishing a Small New England Farmhouse" (*Old Time New England,* Vol. XLVIII). The author pays tribute to these hardy New England farm women: "In those days, people spun

and wove their cloth, knit their own stockings and when I think of mother's cares and labors for her family, I am astonished."

Stephen Walkley, Jr. (1832-1919) wrote in the same article: "I was the youngest of nine children. . . . Each of us had some duty to perform, adapted to our attainments. . . . Mother and the older girls had an uninterrupted chance for work. And, looking back, it seems to me that there was an enormous amount of work to be done. . . . After soap and candle making was over house cleaning commenced . . . there was butter making, cheese making, spinning and weaving."

4. Of seventy-five names, both male and female, taken at random (1780-1860) from the genealogy of the *History of Pembroke,* all except nine were over twenty at the time of marriage. Twenty-seven were married between the ages of twenty-eight and thirty-three. All of these were first marriages.

5. The home of Captain Joseph and Hannah Lovewell Baker was near the Ambrose home. A diary written by a contemporary of Abigail Baker *(Diary of Sarah Connell Ayer, 1805-1835.* Portland, Maine, 1909) is valuable for its descriptions of people and places in Bow and Concord known to the Bakers. Mrs. Ayer writes of canoeing across the Merrimack to Pembroke and of walking across the ice in winter to meeting. She appears to have lived near the Mark Bakers in Bow and mentions Mrs. Baker in her journal.

6. The site and cellar hole of the Ambrose home were rediscovered by the author with the help of the old map of Pembroke included in the *History of Pembroke.*

Nathaniel Ambrose appears to have worked at finishing the meeting house over a period of at least seven years, according to the account book of one Aaron Whittemore, a neighbor. The account book is in the possession of the Whittemore family.

One cannot resist mentioning the following notation, found inside the front cover of Aaron Whittemore's old brown leather account book — evidence as to why the repair of windows was a problem in that day: "Nov. 22, 1808 John and Wm. Garvin and Daniel Boys hove rock to the Meeting House window and broke 9 panes of glass."

7. Letter from Reverend W. Gale, son of Deacon Joseph Gale, who lived near the Ambrose and Baker homes: "I remember well the time when much trouble arose from the introduction of a bass-viol into the singing choir. It was called 'the cursed fiddle.' And at one time, between two Sabbaths, some person, or persons, through prejudice or some other cause, greased the strings of the hateful instrument." "Brief History of the Congregational Church in Pembroke, New Hampshire."

8. An interesting contrast to Mrs. Baker's bedtime hymn is found in a small book, published in 1814 in Newburyport, Massachusetts, called *Hymns for Infant Minds.* It bears out Elizabeth George Speare's comment in her "Child's Life in New England" written for Old Sturbridge Village: "Young readers were sobered and sometimes terrified by constant reminders of the nearness of death and the certainty of judgement." The following stanzas are typical of the tone of the book for "infant minds," and present the religious view which Mark Baker wished to impress upon his children:

> Those who have lov'd Him here below,
>   And pray'd to have their sins forgiven,
> And done His holy will, shall go,
>   Like happy angels, up to heaven.
>
> So while their bodies moulder here,
>   Their souls with God himself shall dwell,
> But always recollect my dear,
>   That wicked people go to hell.
>
> There the good God shall never smile,
>   Nor give them one reviving look;

For since they chose to be so vile,
    He leaves them to the way they took.

Although photographs of Mark Baker and Abigail Tilton and her family are on file at Longyear and in the Archives, and an oil portrait of George Baker hangs in the Longyear Baker Room, no likeness of Mrs. Baker has been found.

9. Archives.

10. A letter of October 9, 1905, from Mrs. Eddy to Daniel White, of Concord, recalls their childhood and Mark Baker's act of neighborliness: "You name the days of our acquaintance. They are hallowed with the golden memories of loving parents, brothers, sisters, friends that I can never cease to love. You speak of some shoes ill made; but you must remember that my father was not a shoemaker and any effort in that direction was pure friendship. I remember the dear old farm and this with all its cares and toil."

The letter was given to the author by the late Mrs. Mary (Fernald) Willis, a granddaughter of Daniel White and daughter of Josiah E. Fernald, Mrs. Eddy's banker in Concord, New Hampshire.

11. Archives.

12. Archives.

Notes: Chapter Six

1. In 1822 Mark Baker became clerk of the Union Church. The church then became the Congregational Church in Bow. It was disbanded in 1829 ("Records of the Union Church of Christ in Bow, 1806-1829," Longyear).

At the New Hampshire Historical Society: "First Methodist Society in Bow (Bow Bog Meeting House), 1826-1867"; *New Hampshire Churches*, Robert Lawrence (1856); "Churches of Merrimac County," Vol. I., William Willard Flint (1931); "Baptist Church Record Book, 1816-1851."

2. Sale of pew to Joseph Baker, April 3, 1805, recorded in bill of sale (Longyear).

3. The author was fortunate to have the opportunity in 1960 of discussing the construction of the old meeting house with the late Arthur Hall, who had recently dismantled it. Although removed from its original site and used as a barn for many years, it was as sound structurally as the year in which it was raised. Other information came from the Bow town record books, as well as the "History of Bow" (N.H.H.S.), part of which is included in the *History of Merrimack and Belknap Counties*, D. Hamilton Hurd (1885). "Churches of Merrimac County" (N.H.H.S.) was also consulted. *Yankee Magazine*, December 1965, contains photos of a meeting house in Sandown, New Hampshire, that greatly resembles the old Bow Meeting House.

4. Mrs. George W. Pierce (Helen Russell) of Sanbornton states that her grandfather, E. Harlow Russell, once boarded with the Mark Bakers at Sanbornton Bridge. What impressed him most during his stay were the "prayers in the morning and grace after meals."

5. Archives.

6. A chaise or carriage was taxable in Bow. Study of tax records for the years of Mark Baker's residence shows that he did not own one. Letters from the girls to George indicate a campaign was waged to convert the father to a means of transportation more elegant than a wagon.

7. *The Christian Science Monitor*, March 10, 1909: "The relic [Mark Baker's gun] is described in detail in *Army and Navy Life, Uncle Sam's Magazine* for March.... [Mr. Baker's] equipment as well as the gun proved to be in fine condition. The former consists of a knapsack, canteen, powder-horn, cartridge-box, belt, and bayonet scabbard. The gun is complete with ramrod and bayonet."

8. A note to Mark Baker from Benjamin Pierce (Longyear) indicates a close relationship. The son, Franklin, asked his friend Albert Baker to make sure that the senior Pierce was well taken care of in the last months of his life. Franklin was then serving in the Senate at Washington. In December 1838, he wrote Albert (N.H.H.S.): "I am anxious to hear again from my dear father. Do write two or three times each week in relation to the state of his health." Albert wrote down the old general's reminiscences at the son's request.

The New Hampshire Historical Society's Pierce Papers show that Franklin considered Albert a close friend as well as business associate.

Notes: Chapter Seven

1. This excerpt is taken from the first printed report of the Bow Superintending School Committee in 1848. This report was written about twenty years after Mary Baker first attended School #3, but it is apparent that conditions had changed little. The report reflects valiant efforts to improve schooling. (In 1964 Bow constructed a half-million-dollar school equipped with the latest educational facilities.)

Clifton Johnson, in his *Old Time Schools and School Books* (1904), states: "The years after the Revolution, till about 1840, form the most picturesque period in our educational history." He paints a vivid picture of the difficulty girls had in obtaining an education in the earliest years, and of the slow gains made over a long period. One early attempt at schooling for young women was so popular, bringing so many girls to the school, that the male experimenters in female education abandoned their project in alarm.

Clifton Johnson tells of one father who was startled to learn his daughter was studying mathematics by herself. The father is said to have remarked to the girl's mother about the

"unnatural" tendency: "Peg, we must put a stop to this or we shall have Mary in a straight-jacket one of these days."

2. Lyford's *History of Concord*, Vol. II, p. 1245. *History of the Schools of Concord* (N.H.H.S.).

A remarkable documentation of the struggle of a talented superintending school committee to bring about reform in the early district schools is given in "A Record of the Doings of the School Committee," Sanbornton, 1840-1852 (Archives). Dyer Sanborn as secretary of the committee reported: "There was great irregularity in attendance . . . this evil I was told, has existed for some years. Still there are several laudable and praise-worthy exceptions." District #17, "Hard Scrabble," the secretary remarked, was "rightly named, too"!

Although there were problems of discipline, children of the day were not without manners. An English traveler noted that the children he passed on the road curtsied or bowed. Courtesy was often a part of the district schooling, known as "making their manners."

3. These incidents in Mary's early school experience are recorded in Irving C. Tomlinson's *Twelve Years with Mary Baker Eddy* (1945).

4. Archives. Mrs. Eddy once demonstrated to a student her knowledge of horses. She explained in detail how to know a good horse as she picked one for her stable. She turned down two horses but decided on a third, and Mrs. Eddy and her new horse "were friends at once."

5. Mary Baker Eddy, *Retrospection and Introspection*, pp. 8, 9.

Notes: Chapter Eight

1. Albert taught school during the fall-winter term of 1829-30. Mark Baker was moderator (chairman) and agent in charge of hiring teachers for the school during the years 1830-32. The school term ran from ten to twenty weeks. The length of time appears to have depended upon the availability of teachers and funds (Record book, School #3, Bow).

Walter H. Small, writing in 1914 *(Early New England Schools)*, stated that the early New England primary school was "not a popular institution; it was conceived, supported and perpetuated by the few . . . its course in most towns was erratic, and yet . . . a marvelous institution, the bedrock of future educational systems."

2. *New Hampshire Patriot and State Gazette,* November 4, 1841.

3. "History of Bow" (N.H.H.S.).

4. Catalogue for Pembroke Academy, 1832.

5. Archives.

6. Albert to George, October 15, 1837.

7. Roy F. Nichols, *Franklin Pierce* (1958). Also, an address by David Cross before the New Hampshire Bar Association, 1909 (N.H.H.S.).

8. According to Elmer Ellsworth Brown, in *The Making of Our Middle Schools* (1903), the Lindley Murray *Grammar* (published originally in 1795) gave the first definite direction to the systematic study of the English language in the United States. Murray's *Grammar* was freely adapted, abridged, or simplified by many authors. For several decades it provided the basic material for instruction in grammar.

Murray's aim was the student's mastery of "the art of speaking and writing the English language with propriety," and this was to be attained through practical composition, oral reading and declamation, and the study of masterpieces of literature. Murray's *English Reader* carried the student a step further in his study of the subject. The *Grammar* was the most influential book in its field.

9. Archives.

10. Archives.

11. Mary Baker Eddy's notebooks, Archives and Longyear.

12. Mary Baker Eddy, *Retrospection*, p. 10.

13. Albert to Mary, March 27, 1837.

Notes: Chapter Nine

1. The construction of the Bow Bog Meeting House can be placed between 1828 and 1834. It may well have been under way for several years, as these projects were not always completed rapidly. "Records of Bow Bog Meeting House, 1827-1836" and "Churches of Merrimac County" (N.H.H.S.).

At the turn of the century Mrs. Eddy donated a bell for the steeple.

In recent years the Methodists left the Bow Bog Meeting House for a new church building. A nonsectarian society was formed by local townspeople to save the historic structure.

2. "Records, Parish Committee, Abraham Burnham's Society in Pembroke" (1808). "Records of the Pembroke Society for Reformation of Morals" (1815). "Book of Records for the Society of the South Meeting House in Pembroke" (1807). (N.H.H.S.)

3. Mrs. Eddy referred to the three ministers she knew as a child in Bow in her *Message to The Mother Church for 1901*, p. 32. The Reverend Abraham Burnham seems to have been popular in Bow and evidently preached there many times. It is recorded that he often moderated the church meetings. It was probably at these times that he stayed overnight with the Bakers. This was recalled in later years by Mrs. Eddy when she revisited the old homestead (personal notes of Mrs. Mary Willis).

4. "Discourse at the Funeral of Rev. Abraham Burnham," Reverend Daniel J. Noyes.

5. Mary Baker Eddy, *Message to The Mother Church for 1901*, p. 32.

6. "Brief History of the Congregational Church in Pembroke." "Manual of the Congregational Church," Pembroke. *History of Pembroke.*

7. The description of the Reverend Dr. Bouton and the Congregational Church is drawn from the following sources: Bouton's own excellent *History of Concord* written during a ministry of 42 years; the *Diary of Sarah Connell Ayer, 1805-1835; New Hampshire Churches; History and Manual, First Congregational Church, Concord, 1730-1907* (1907).

8. Mary Baker Eddy, *The First Church of Christ, Scientist, and Miscellany,* p. 147.

9. "A Sketch of the Character and Life-Work of Rev. Nathaniel Bouton, D.D., 1825-1867," by his son, John Bell Bouton (N.H.H.S.), read at the evening service of the church, April 27, 1902, by Mrs. Arthur E. Clarke (Martha Cilley Bouton, his daughter).

Notes: Chapter Ten

1. Albert to Mary, March 27, 1837.

2. William G. McLoughlin, Jr., in his *Modern Revivalism* (1959), indicates that the protracted meetings had their sources in the three- and four-day camp meetings on the southwest frontier. Opinion on the value of such revivals has been divided. An English visitor to the United States wrote in 1828 of the protracted meetings: "They are addressed by their preachers, with the most terrific warnings. . . . I have seen men in such agony, as might easily be mistaken . . . for the remorse of a murderer. . . . People are actually questioned concerning their most secret and delicate feelings *in a crowd,* and it is considered a mark of pride or obduracy to decline so open a disclosure." (Orville Dewey, *Revivals of Religion,* 1828.)

However, Joshua Bradley, writing in 1819 (*Accounts of Religious Revival in the United States*), observed: "At every meeting some came forward and told what the Lord had done for their souls . . . no disorder appeared; only one spoke at a time with the greatest calmness, and yet with fervency."

Another Englishman, the Reverend Calvin Colton, felt the revivals accomplished good (*History and Character of American Revival of Religion,* 1832). Of particular interest, especially in view of the fact that Mary Baker appears to have "come forward" at the age of 12, is the author's description of a scene following a revival: "[The] parents with their children, presented themselves . . . in the broad aisle of the church . . . candidates in fellowship and privileges of church."

One of the best indications of the significance attached to the protracted meeting is the statement made in reference to the Massachusetts Bay Colony by Gaius Glenn Atkins and Frederick L. Fagley in their *History of American Congregationalism* (1942): "Religion was their only avocation and that they took with a seriousness beyond exaggeration. Indeed their concern for their souls made it their real vocation. Were they not wayfarers seeking Heaven Gate and always in peril of missing it?"

3. The record book for the First Congregational Church indicates clearly that only adults were listed as members, although it is evident that young people were encouraged to come forward at revivals. Joshua Bradley describes one revival in New Hampshire: "The happy subjects of this work have been principally youths from 14 to 25 years of age. One of only 11 years obtained a Comfortable hope."

The *Sabbath School Treasury* (Massachusetts Sabbath School Union, 1832) reported: ". . . powerful revivals . . . have blessed our churches, gathering a much larger number of hopeful converts from among our Sabbath school children, than from an equal number of individuals of any other class or age."

According to Henry C. Fish, writing in *The Handbook of Revivals* (1874), there was a "hesitancy" to receive those under sixteen, and "a vast amount of skepticism on the subject." This was perhaps a logical conclusion

177

for a time in which young people did not usually leave home and often did not marry until their early twenties.

4. Luke 2:42-52.

5. Mary Baker Eddy, *Retrospection*, p. 13; and *Miscellany*, p. 311.

6. *Diary of Sarah Connell Ayer*. "Records of the First Congregational Church, Concord" (N.H.H.S.).

7. Mary actually joined the church when she was seventeen, after another struggle over predestination. (See page 88.) In later years, it seems that the two experiences were so closely connected in her thought that we cannot be sure today which incidents belong to the earlier experience, which to the later.

Notes: Chapter Eleven

1. Baker letters, 1835-36.

2. Baker letters and George Baker's "Journal."

3. Lyford's *History of Concord*.

4. To send one sheet of letter paper 400 miles cost twenty-five cents, a large sum in that day.

5. George Waldo Browne, *History of Hillsborough, New Hampshire, 1735-1921* (1921).

6. The story is told in Hillsborough that Abigail helped the Pierces keep house and baked a very special and delicious gingerbread.

7. Harrison C. Baldwin, *History of Hillsborough, 1921-1963* (1963).

8. Archives.

Notes: Chapter Twelve

1. Baker letters.

2. Longyear and Archives.

3. *History of Sanbornton*. Map of Sanbornton (1858), picture-map (1884), photograph of Main Street (1860), in Archives.

4. Henrietta H. Williams, "The Founder of Christian Science," *New England Magazine*, November 1899.

5. *History of Sanbornton*. Record book of the Sanbornton School Committee, Archives.

The Baker home was located in School District #1. At this time, according to the record book and the town history, the district was divided into two sections, the Bridge and Tin Corner. Priscilla Clement, Mary's friend, lived at Tin Corner, about a mile from the Baker home. Sister Abby was teaching at the Bridge school but living in town rather than at home, so the Bridge school was apparently not located conveniently near the Bakers.

6. Priscilla Clement's letters to Mary are at Longyear Foundation. The Augusta Holmes letters are in the Archives of The Mother Church.

7. Sarah Bodwell's memory book, Longyear.

8. *History of Sanbornton; History of Merrimack and Belknap Counties;* Baker letters. The town of Sanbornton was divided in 1869. The section known as the Bridge was named Tilton, in honor of the Tilton family, which held a prominent position in town affairs.

Notes: Chapter Thirteen

1. Record book of Sanbornton Academy, 1820-1851 (N.H.H.S.). *History of Sanbornton*.

2. Record book of the Sanbornton School Committee, 1840-1852. Abraham Bodwell, Dyer Sanborn, and Dr. John Carr made up the committee. The record, kept by Mr. Sanborn who was clerk, indicates that the committee was attempting to set standards in the Sanbornton schools higher than those generally found elsewhere. Several lengthy reports recommend what must have been considered sweeping reforms.

3. *Mary Baker Eddy Mentioned Them* (1961), pp. 38, 39. "Manual of the Congregational Church of Tilton" (1922).

4. *History of Sanbornton. History of Boscawen, 1733-1878.* Mr. Corser was a native of Boscawen.

5. "An Account of the Seventy-Fifth Anniversary of the Congregational Church of Northfield and Tilton" (1897).

6. *Ibid.*

7. Record book of Sanbornton Academy (N.H.H.S.).

8. Memoirs of Emma Easton Newman (Longyear), regarding conversations with Enoch Corser's son, Bartlett, who was related to Mrs. Newman.

9. Sibyl Wilbur, *The Life of Mary Baker Eddy* (1941), p. 33.

10. Clifford P. Smith, *Historical Sketches* (1941), p. 31.

11. Luther Pilsbury (Martha Baker's husband) to Mary, May 17, 1848.

12. It is difficult to ascertain the exact nature of the illnesses as noted in the family letters. Even where descriptions are given, the terminology is different from modern medical language. Acute dyspepsia and a spinal weakness seem to have been Mary's problems for some years until her discovery of Christian Science.

13. The town of Northfield lies on the southern bank of the Winnepesaukee River, directly opposite Sanbornton Bridge.

14. Although the old records for the Sanbornton (Tilton) church are lost, photocopies were made at the turn of the century of the portion showing Mary Baker's membership (Longyear and Archives).

15. "Lydia Ann" to Augusta Holmes, August 21, 1838, Archives.

16. Deacon Elias Abbott was held in great respect and affection by his townspeople. Mrs. Eddy's letter referring to this experience was written to the Tilton (Sanbornton) Congregational Church on the occasion of its seventy-fifth anniversary, in 1897. It was read during the anniversary program and was reproduced in *New England Magazine,* November 1899.

Notes: Chapter Fourteen

1. "An Account of the Seventy-Fifth Anniversary of the Congregational Church of Northfield and Tilton, New Hampshire."

2. Wilbur, *Mary Baker Eddy,* p. 34.

3. Papers at Longyear Foundation confirm the story of Lyman Durgin, and the small New Testament given to him by Mary Baker is exhibited there. The *History of Sanbornton* gives additional information about the Durgin family.

4. Certain inaccuracies concerning Mrs. Eddy's education have resulted from the similarity in the names of the two academies: Sanbornton Academy and Woodman-Sanbornton Academy. The first was located at the Bridge and the second at the Square. Both academies were sometimes referred to merely as Sanbornton Academy, or the Academy. Dyer Sanborn was principal, at different times, at both academies. However, Sarah Bodwell was preceptress only at Woodman, as it is referred to hereafter.

Miss Bodwell's father, Abraham, was a leading figure at Woodman Academy throughout the school's existence, from 1826-1857. Mrs. Joseph Bodwell, whose late husband was a direct descendant, helped the author greatly by sifting old records to obtain a complete tax record of Mark Baker's residence in Sanbornton.

5. Several dozen catalogs for academies in New Hampshire at this period have been examined. *The Making of Our Middle Schools* is an excellent source. The author describes the common practice of mixing college and high school level courses. It was this, along with Mary Baker's tutoring and aptitude for self-instruction, which bears out her own estimate that her education was "most thorough" (cf. Tomlinson).

6. Dyer H. Sanborn over the course of a lifetime was associated with six academies in New Hampshire and Massachusetts. His education was gained from advanced academy courses and self-instruction, but he was given an honorary degree by Dartmouth College for his work in education. His educational theories, careful discipline, and choice of curriculum were advanced for his day. The record book of the Sanbornton School Committee for the years 1840-1847, when he was secretary, gives an indication of his professional outlook.

He was obviously the instigator of reform in the district schools, as well as at the academies. Such reform was not always welcomed by parents. In the catalog of 1842 for Sanbornton Academy he warned: "The prospective excuses of ill health, bad weather, and distance from school should receive no hearing from the indulgent parent." And in the school record book he observed: "No one will entrust a favorite horse to a careless, reckless driver, yet many called wise will entrust children to the care of an incompetent instructor."

Sanborn was at one time representative for the town to the New Hampshire state legislature. It was he who recommended Mary's brother George for the position of aide to the governor.

7. Catalog Woodman-Sanbornton Academy, 1839. It states: "A Rhetorical Exercise and Composition are required of the Young Ladies, alternately, every Wednesday afternoon." The author has an extensive collection of textbooks and catalogs of this period, including those described here.

8. In 1838 Sarah Jane Bodwell married Colonel Charles Lane, a member of the Board of Trustees of Woodman Academy. In 1841 he became publisher of the *Belknap Gazette,* in Laconia, then known as Meredith Bridge.

Notes: Chapter Fifteen

1. *New Hampshire Journal of the Senate and House,* June Session, 1839.

2. Pierce Papers (N.H.H.S.).

3. A Concord coach in splendid condition is exhibited in the rotunda of the New Hampshire Historical Society. The coach was used throughout the United States. Another original is in the History Room at the main office, Wells Fargo Bank, San Francisco, California.

4. Mary Baker Eddy, *Poems,* p. 64.

5. Three letters written to Augusta Holmes and signed "Mary" have for many years been considered authentic although posted from Meredith Bridge (now Laconia). These letters were the basis for the statement that Mary attended Plymouth Academy in northern New Hampshire. However, research by the author, in conjunction with the Archives of The Mother Church, suggests strongly that these letters were not written to Augusta by Mary Baker but by another Mary. The Bakers never lived elsewhere than in Bow and Sanbornton, as is proven by tax records. Thus there seems at this time no firm evidence for believing that Mary Baker attended Plymouth Academy.

6. Mary Baker Eddy, *Miscellaneous Writings,* 363:27-29.

7. Material at Longyear Foundation seems to indicate that Mary Baker acted as correspondent for the *Belknap Gazette.* Longyear has a clipping of the newspaper article entitled "The Phalanx, a Company of Light Infantry," which describes the forming of a typical group of local militia. The description of Muster Day is taken from the *History of Sanbornton.*

8. *New Hampshire Journals of the Senate and House;* and Pierce Papers (N.H.H.S.). Roy F. Nichols, *Franklin Pierce.*

9. Smith, *Historical Sketches,* p. 27.

10. The family papers and letters carefully kept by George Baker throw much light on the

Baker family history and manner of living. Most of them are included in the Longyear Collection. A New York antique dealer found the bulk of the letters and papers in a rawhide trunk in the attic of George Baker's home in Tilton after Mathy Rand Baker passed away in 1909. Mary's letters discovered at this time, including "the second I ever wrote," were reproduced in *Munsey's Magazine*, April 1911.

Notes: Chapter Sixteen

1. Record book of the Sanbornton School Committee 1840-1852: "Dyer H. Sanborn visited Martha S. Baker's school in Dis. No. 1 at Sandbornton Bridge. The Discipline of the School was excellent. Miss Baker exhibited the traits of an able, efficient, and competent teacher. Whole No. of Scholars, 70. . . . There was a deficiency of Books, in this School, especially in the primary branches of education. This had been partially remedied by the enterprise of its teacher. This remark respecting deficiency of books, is true, with regard to most Schools in town. Scholars, by the intercession of their teachers, have in some instances, prevailed upon their parents to procure books for them."

2. Catalogue of Sandbornton Academy, 1842.

3. Lyman P. Powell, *Mary Baker Eddy: A Life Size Portrait* (1950), p. 283.

4. George Washington Glover to George Baker, May 19, 1841, Longyear.

5. Mary Baker's "Journal of a Trip to the White Hills in July, 1843," Archives.

6. Both poems were recorded by Mary in one of her notebooks (No. 2), Archives.

7. The statement "I married young the one I loved" was made by Mrs. Eddy in a letter to Clara Louise Burnham, September 21, 1902 (Longyear).

Corban Curtice had replaced Enoch Corser as minister of the Congregational Church. He was a young man at the time of his appointment, and quickly became a friend of the Baker family.

Notes: Chapter Seventeen

1. One of Mary Baker Eddy's notebooks (No. 2, in Archives) includes the text of these "toasts."

2. This review and other compositions written at about the same time are also included in Mrs. Eddy's notebooks.

3. Robert Peel, *Mary Baker Eddy: The Years of Discovery* (1966), p. 72.

4. Mary Baker Eddy, *Miscellany*, p. 331. "Major Glover's record as a Mason," *Freemason's Monthly Magazine*, 1845.

5. "Journal of the Journey from Wilmington," Archives.

6. Peel, *The Years of Discovery*, p. 78.

7. See Mary Baker Eddy, *Retrospection*, 24:7.

8. Record book of the Sanbornton School Committee, 1840-1852.

9. Catalogs of the New Hampshire Conference Seminary, 1845-1849.

10. Mrs. Eddy's notebooks (No. 2), Archives.

11. "Immortality of the Soul" by Mary Baker Glover, published in *The Covenant*, May 1847.

12. Mary Baker Glover to Mathy Rand, March 1848, Longyear.

Notes: Chapter Eighteen

1. In a few years, the Tilton mill doubled in size and made a reputation for itself in the manufacture of Tilton Tweeds. At her husband's death some years later, Abby took over the management of the mill and was considered one of the wealthiest women in Tilton at the time of her passing in 1886. She was also well known for her many charitable contributions.

Alexander Tilton's cousin Charles, who made a fortune in the West, gave liberally to the town. He donated statuary, an island park, a town hall, and a magnificent and enormous arch on a hill overlooking the village.

2. Not a great deal is known of John Bartlett, but it is possible to trace his whereabouts through Mary's letters and the catalogs of the schools he attended. The alumni bulletins for the New Hampshire Conference Seminary list his addresses from the time of his enrollment until his trip to California.

3. It has been believed that Mrs. Baker passed on after moving to her new home. However, careful study of newspapers and letters indicates either that the house was not completed before she died or her illness prevented the move.

4. John Bartlett died December 11, 1849. Mary kept a copy of the notice in her scrapbook (Archives).

5. Mark Baker to George, May 31, 1850 (Longyear): "I have Martha and children and Mary to maintain and a hired Girl to give a dollar a week so I must with might to keep from poverty right off."

6. Mary to George (evidently in 1850), a year after their mother's death (Longyear): "This anniversary has indeed passed — but the absent and the dead — where are they? Not with us as we gather slowly and silently around the table and at evening with deeper memories separated! Our dear sister band is yet unbroken, but ere another Thanksgiving we may be among the distant or quiet dead and life's fitful fever o'er."

7. At least one faintly cheering note was struck during this difficult time. Two of Mary's poems were chosen to be included in the New Hampshire anthology *Gems for You*. It was an elegantly bound gift book, a combination of poetry and prose from New Hampshire authors. Horace Greeley, the American newspaper editor who gave the advice, "Go West, young man, go West," was one of Mary's fellow contributors.

8. Mary Baker Eddy, *Retrospection*, p. 20.

9. Mary Baker Eddy, *Science and Health with Key to the Scriptures*, 66:30-1.

Notes: **Chapter Nineteen**

1. Baker letters, Longyear.

2. Archives.

3. Archives.

4. *The Christian Science Hymnal* (1931), hymn #207.

5. *History of Sanbornton.*

6. Baker letters, Longyear.

7. Baker letters, Longyear.

8. Archives.

Notes: **Chapter Twenty**

1. Mrs. Sarah C. Turner's memoirs are deposited in the Archives of The Mother Church.

Women were beginning to be heard in the church and in the community, although there was still a long road ahead before women's suffrage came to pass. Speaking in 1897 at the Seventy-Fifth Anniversary of the Congregational Church in Tilton (Sanbornton Bridge), Mrs. L. R. H. Cross recalled a scene at the Sanbornton church during a revival service that might well have had reference to Mary Baker Glover:

"How vividly the scene comes before me! Our pastor said, 'Will some brother lead in prayer?' whereupon [a woman in the congregation] rose and said, 'Why not a sister pray?'

"She then uttered one of the most impassioned appeals to the throne of grace I ever listened to.

"The same question has often recurred to me, since, and I am rejoiced that the sisters may, as well as the brethren, follow the dictates of their conscience, in either praying or speaking, here.

"I am quite sure, before you celebrate your centennial, there will be a deaconess on your list, and also a female superintendent of your Sunday-school."

— And there was.

2. Elmyra Smith Wilson reminiscences, Archives.

3. Mary Baker Eddy, *Science and Health,* p. 156.

Homeopathic kits and manuals for home doctoring were popular at this time. Mary Patterson doubtless had a complete selection of homeopathic medicines since she was especially interested in the subject.

One of these home kits is included in the Smaus family's collection of old New England artifacts. Small bottles of various pills and potions are lined up neatly in one half of a black leather case, and a book of directions on the mixing of remedies for various ailments fits into the other half. A "Pocket Manual of Homeopathic Practice" was available to combine with the "Homeopathic Family Medicine Case." The homeopathic chemist sold these cases for prices ranging from $1.50 (12 medicines) to $8.00 (86 medicines, complete).

4. Martha's letters at this time show her anguish over the dilemma the unpaid debt was causing this most tenderhearted of the Baker family. Certainly it was because she was convinced the situation could only worsen that she foreclosed. Martha's last years (she died in 1884) were spent in Kansas with Ellen and her husband, Edwin Philbrook, who was, according to the *History of Sanbornton,* "an eminent school teacher."

5. Mary Baker Eddy, *Miscellany,* 149:31-2.

6. Wilbur, *Mary Baker Eddy,* p. 70.

7. Reminiscences of Grace Chard, Archives.

8. At the age of seventeen, in 1861, Georgy enlisted with the Union Army for three years. He reenlisted in 1864, and was discharged for disability in 1865. He was severely wounded in battle at Corinth, Mississippi, in April 1862, at the famous battle of Shiloh. (Ambrose Genealogy, John Lee Ambrose, about 1909, N.H.H.S.)

9. The author is indebted to Allison W. Phinney for research and conversations concerning Phineas Parkhurst Quimby. See also accounts in Smith, *Historical Sketches;* Powell, *Mary Baker Eddy;* DeWitt John, *The Christian Science Way of Life* (1962); Robert Peel, *Mary Baker Eddy: The Years of Discovery.*

10. As Quimby worked with a patient, he often dipped his hands in a bowl of water and then rubbed the person's head or he asked the patient to drink a glass of water. Sometimes he simply talked with the patient, firmly explaining his views of the way the mind worked on the body, producing heat and cold, pain in this place or that.

In a sketch referring to himself characteristically in the third person, Quimby once wrote: "In this way, Quimby went on taking up and explaining almost every idea he [the patient] ever had and putting a different construction, till R. thought he did not know anything." (Library of Congress, Quimby Papers)

Horatio Dresser in *The Quimby Manuscripts* (1921) observes: "The nearest he [Quimby] comes to a description of the process is in the following illustration. . . ." Dresser then quotes from Quimby's writings a passage which includes the statement: "Then his feelings in regard to the disease, which are health and strength, are daguerreotyped on the receptive-plate of the patient." It is instructive to compare Mrs. Eddy's statements on the nature of Christian Science healing in her *Miscellaneous Writings,* 96:28-14.

11. Peel, *The Years of Discovery,* pp. 189 and 349.

Notes: Chapter Twenty-One

1. Mary M. Patterson to Mrs. Williams, March 8, 1863, Archives. See Peel, *The Years of Discovery,* p. 171.

2. Wilbur, *Mary Baker Eddy,* p. 103.

3. Letter of Sarah G. Crosby to Horace T. Wentworth, November 14, 1903, Archives.

4. Powell, *A Life Size Portrait,* p. 105.

5. Wilbur, *Mary Baker Eddy*, p. 118.

6. Statement by George Newhall, August 29, 1920, Longyear. See also Smith's *Historical Sketches*, p. 55.

7. A description of the accident was given in the *Lynn Reporter*, February 3, 1866. The account was as follows:

> Mrs. Mary M. Patterson, of Swampscott, fell upon the ice near the corner of Market and Oxford Streets, on Thursday evening, and was severely injured. She was taken up in an insensible condition and carried to the residence of S. M. Bubier, Esq., near by, where she was kindly cared for during the night. Dr. Cushing, who was called, found her injuries to be internal, and of a very serious nature, inducing spasms and intense suffering. She was removed to her home in Swampscott yesterday afternoon, though in a very critical condition.

8. Archives.

9. Smith, *Historical Sketches*, p. 58.

10. Mary Baker Eddy, *Miscellaneous Writings*, 24:14-18.

11. Mary Baker Eddy, *Retrospection*, 23:14-15, 22-24.

Notes: Chapter Twenty-Two

1. Mary Baker Eddy, *Retrospection*, 27:21-26. See also *The Christian Science Journal*, Vol. 53, May 1935, pp. 110, 111 (reprint of Mrs. Eddy's statement from the *Journal*, June 1887).

2. Mary Baker Eddy, *Retrospection*, 23:7-14.

3. *Ibid.*, 31:13-19 and 34:1-4.

4. Kenneth Hufford, "Mary Baker Eddy and the Stoughton Years," p. 23 (a Longyear Foundation historical pamphlet, 1963).

5. Mary Baker Eddy, *Retrospection*, 26:12-16.

6. *Ibid.*, 25:29-3.

7. Mary Baker Eddy, *Miscellaneous Writings*, 380:7-13.

8. Mary Baker Eddy, *Science and Health*, viii:28-32.

9. Mary's closeness to her mother is evident in her poem called "To My Mother in Heaven," published in the *New Hampshire Patriot*, December 20, 1849 (Archives).

10. Wilbur, *Mary Baker Eddy*, p. 145.

11. A young man who had just returned from hearing Mrs. Eddy speak at a Sunday morning service wrote his mother, "I don't wonder that she is loved, — she is all love." (Reprinted in *The Christian Science Journal*, Vol. XIII, July 1895.)

12. Wilbur, *Mary Baker Eddy*, pp. 140, 141.

13. *Ibid.*, pp. 142, 143.

14. Mary Baker Eddy, *Retrospection*, 24:7-11. Mary Baker Eddy, *Miscellany*, 348:17-21.

15. *Ibid.*, 348:21-27.

Notes: Chapter Twenty-Three

1. Statement by Hiram Crafts, December 19, 1901, Archives.

2. Hugh A. Studdert-Kennedy, *Mrs. Eddy* (1947), p. 141

3. Mary Baker Eddy, *Science and Health*, ix:29-2.

4. Mary Baker Eddy, *Poems*, 8:15.

5. *Ibid.*, 9:8-11.

6. Wilbur, *Mary Baker Eddy*, p. 134.

7. Mary Baker Eddy, *Miscellany*, 313:27-29.

8. Mary Baker Eddy, *Science and Health*, 109:15-16.

9. Mary Baker Eddy, *Miscellany*, 302:18-20.

10. The healing was described by Martha Rand Baker in an interview given to a slightly skeptical inquirer some years later. (Reminiscences of Mrs. Addie Towns Arnold, Archives)

11. Archives.

12. Mary to George Baker, November 1850, Longyear.

13. Hufford, "Mary Baker Eddy and the Stoughton Years," p. 26.

14. Mary Baker Eddy, *Retrospection*, 35:4-10.

15. Letter to the *Lynn Transcript*, January 20, 1872.

16. Letter to the *Lynn Transcript*, February 3, 1872. See Peel, *The Years of Discovery*, p. 272.

17. Mary Baker Eddy, *Science and Health*, 581:4, 5.

18. Archives.

19. Archives.

20. The first chapter of the first edition of *Science and Health* was called "Natural Science." Later, the chapters were rearranged and others were added. The first chapter of *Science and Health* now is called "Prayer."

21. The recollection of William Scott, quoted by Alfred Farlow in "Historical Facts Concerning Mary Baker Eddy and Christian Science," pp. 107, 108, an unpublished manuscript (Archives).

22. Wilbur, *Mary Baker Eddy*, p. 201.

23. On September 5, 1874, the manuscript was first placed in the hands of the printer. Peel, *The Years of Discovery*, p. 283.

24. Wilbur, *Mary Baker Eddy*, pp. 203, 204.

25. E. Mary Ramsay, *Christian Science and Its Discoverer*, p. 74.

26. Mary Baker Eddy, *Science and Health*, vii:1-4. The opening sentences were worded a little differently in the first edition of the book.

Notes: Epilogue

1. Mary Baker Eddy, *Science and Health*, 361:21, 22.

2. Mary Baker Eddy, "A True Man," *Retrospection*, p. 42.

3. Mary Baker Eddy, *Manual of The Mother Church, The First Church of Christ, Scientist, in Boston, Massachusetts*, p. 17.

4. Robert Peel, *Christian Science: Its Encounter with American Culture* (1958), p. 52.

5. A complete listing of the Lesson-Sermon or Bible Lesson subjects is given in each issue of the *Christian Science Quarterly*, p. iii.

6. In a startlingly prophetic passage Mrs. Eddy wrote, in *Science and Health*, 125:21:

> The seasons will come and go with changes of time and tide, cold and heat, latitude and longtitude. The agriculturist will find that these changes cannot affect his crops. "As a vesture shalt Thou change them and they shall be changed." The mariner will have dominion over the atmosphere and the great deep, over the fish of the sea and the fowls of the air. The astronomer will no longer look up to the stars, — he will look out from them upon the universe; and the florist will find his flower before its seed.

See also Chapter Five, "Why Call it Science?" in *The Christian Science Way of Life* by DeWitt John.

7. Mary Baker Eddy, *Message for 1900*, 9:20-22.

8. Mary Baker Eddy, *Science and Health*, 256:24.

9. See Erwin D. Canham's *Commitment to Freedom: The Story of The Christian Science Monitor* (1958), pp. 10-13.

10. Mrs. Daisette McKenzie told this charming story to the author.

11. Letters from George Glover to his mother (N.H.H.S.).

12. Smith, *Historical Sketches*, p. 70.

13. *The Story of Christian Science Wartime*

Activities, 1939-1946 (1947), p. 402 comments: "a great-grandson of Mary Baker Eddy . . . served in the [United States] Navy and also as a Christian Science Volunteer Wartime Worker. The wife of another great-grandson of Mrs. Eddy was in the WAC [United States Women's Army Corps]. Both are earnest students of Christian Science."

14. Reminiscences of William Lyman Johnson, Archives.

15. Mrs. Eddy returned to live in Chestnut Hill, Massachusetts, in January 1908. (See Powell's *Mary Baker Eddy*, p. 214.) From that vantage point, at the age of eighty-seven, she founded and gave daily attention to *The Christian Science Monitor*. See Erwin Canham's *Commitment to Freedom*, p. 54. Mrs. Eddy passed on December 3, 1910.

16. Mary Baker Eddy, *Miscellany*, 366:7-14.

17. Accounts in Concord newspapers, also the *Christian Science Sentinel*, Vol. V, July 4, 1903, pp. 696-698.

18. The grandson of the "lady with the big hat," William Colby, a resident of Concord, recounted his grandmother's counsel to him in a conversation with the author.

19. Mrs. Mary Willis of Concord, the sister of one of the girls in the pony cart, remembered the scene and described it for the author during a pleasant visit.

20. Concord newspapers, also the *Christian Science Sentinel*, Vol. V, July 4, 1903, pp. 696-698.

21. From the diary of Alice Noble Converse, through the kind permission of her son, Gordon Noble Converse.

22. Mary Baker Eddy, *Science and Health*, 236:29-32.

23. Reminiscences of Miss Julia S. Bartlett. Archives.

Bibliography for Further Reading

While most of the research for this book has been based on original sources or material that is out of print, the books listed below are generally available. They have been drawn on by the author and will be useful for enrichment reading. A complete bibliography is on file with the Archives of The Mother Church.

Works by Mary Baker Eddy

Published by the Trustees under the Will of Mary Baker Eddy in Boston, Massachusetts
Science and Health with Key to the Scriptures
Prose Works other than Science and Health. This book includes the following which are available in separate volumes: *Christian Healing; Christian Science versus Pantheism; Message to The Mother Church for 1900; Message to The Mother Church for 1901; Message to The Mother Church for 1902; Miscellaneous Writings; No and Yes; Pulpit and Press; Retrospection and Introspection; Rudimental Divine Science; The First Church of Christ, Scientist, and Miscellany; The People's Idea of God;* and *Unity of Good.*
Manual of The Mother Church, The First Church of Christ, Scientist, in Boston, Massachusetts
Poems, Including Christ and Christmas

Other Works Related to Christian Science

A Century of Christian Science Healing. Boston: The Christian Science Publishing Society, 1966.
Armstrong, Joseph. *The Mother Church.* Boston: The Christian Science Publishing Society, 1937.
Beasley, Norman. *The Cross and the Crown: The History of Christian Science.* New York: Duell, Sloan and Pearce, 1952. *The Continuing Spirit: The Story of Christian Science Since 1910.* New York: Duell,

Sloan and Pearce, 1956. *Mary Baker Eddy.* New York: Duell, Sloan and Pearce, 1963.

Canham, Erwin D. *Commitment to Freedom: The Story of The Christian Science Monitor.* Boston: Houghton Mifflin Co., 1958.

Hay, Ella H. *A Child's Life of Mary Baker Eddy.* Boston: The Christian Science Publishing Society, 1942.

John, DeWitt, and Canham, Erwin D. *The Christian Science Way of Life* with *A Christian Scientist's Life.* Englewood Cliffs, N. J.: Prentice-Hall, Inc., 1962.

Johnston, Julia Michael. *Mary Baker Eddy: Her Mission and Triumph.* Boston: The Christian Science Publishing Society, 1946.

Mary Baker Eddy Mentioned Them. Boston: The Christian Science Publishing Society, 1961.

Orcutt, William Dana. *Mary Baker Eddy and Her Books.* Boston: The Christian Science Publishing Society, 1950.

Peel, Robert. *Christian Science: Its Encounter with American Culture.* New York: Holt, Rinehart and Winston, 1958. *Mary Baker Eddy: The Years of Discovery.* New York: Holt, Rinehart and Winston, 1966.

Powell, Lyman P. *Mary Baker Eddy: A Life Size Portrait.* Boston: The Christian Science Publishing Society, 1950.

Ramsay, E. Mary. *Christian Science and Its Discoverer.* Boston: The Christian Science Publishing Society, 1935.

Smith, Clifford P. *Historical Sketches.* Boston: The Christian Science Publishing Society, 1941.

Tomlinson, Irving C. *Twelve Years with Mary Baker Eddy.* Boston: The Christian Science Publishing Society, 1945.

We Knew Mary Baker Eddy. (Series of three books) Boston: The Christian Science Publishing Society, 1943, 1950, 1953.

Wilbur, Sibyl. *The Life of Mary Baker Eddy.* Boston: The Christian Science Publishing Society, 1941.

Williamson, Margaret. *The Mother Church Extension.* Boston: The Christian Science Publishing Society, 1939.

Books of General Interest and Background

Baldwin, Harrison C. *History of Hillsborough, 1921-1963.* Peterborough, New Hampshire: Transcript Printing Co., 1963.

Beardsley, Frank G. *A History of American Revivals.* American Tract Society, 1904.

Bickford, Elizabeth. *The Little Girl of Long Ago.* Boston: Bruce Humphries, Inc., 1956.

Blood, Grace Holbrook. *Manchester on the Merrimack.* Manchester, N. H.: Lew A. Cummings Co., 1948.

Brown, Elmer E. *The Making of Our Middle Schools.* New York: Longman's Green and Co., 1926.

Browne, George W. *History of Hillsborough, New Hampshire, 1735-1921.* Manchester, New Hampshire: Published by the town, 1921.

Earle, Alice Morse. *Home Life in Colonial Days.* New York: The Macmillan Co., 1917.

Gingrich, Gerald Ira. *Protestant Revival Yesterday and Today.* New York: Exposition Press, 1959.

Johnson, Clifton. *Old Time Schools and School Books.* New York: Macmillan, 1904; Dover Publications, 1963.

McLoughlin, William G., Jr. *Modern Revivalism.* New York: Ronald Press, 1959.

Mussey, Barrows. *Old New England.* New York: A. A. Wyn, Inc., 1946.

Nearing, Helen and Scott. *The Maple Sugar Book.* New York: The John Day Co., 1950.

New Hampshire: A Guide to the Granite State. American Guide Series. W.P.A. Writers Project. Boston: Houghton Mifflin Co., 1938.

Nichols, Roy Franklin. *Franklin Pierce: Young Hickory of the Granite Hills.* Second edition revised. Philadelphia: The University of Pennsylvania Press, 1958.

Nye, Russel Blaine. *The Cultural Life of the New Nation, 1776-1830*. New York: Harper, 1960.

Rawson, Marion Nicholl. *Candle Days*. New York-London: The Century Co., 1927.

Sloan, Eric. *American Barns and Covered Bridges*. New York: Wilfred Funk, Inc., 1954. *Diary of An Early American Boy*. New York: Wilfred Funk, Inc., 1962.

Tunis, Edward. *Colonial Living*. Cleveland and New York: The World Publishing Co., 1957.

Booklets

Atkins, Gaius Glenn and Phillips, Helen E. *An Adventure in Liberty. A Short History of the Congregational Christian Churches*. Boston-Chicago: The Pilgrim Press, 1942.

Hufford, Kenneth. *Mary Baker Eddy and the Stoughton Years*. Longyear Foundation, 1963.

Lutz, Alma. *The Birthplace of Christian Science*. Longyear Foundation, 1935. *The Rumney Years*, Longyear Foundation, 1940.

Old Sturbridge Village Booklet Series: There are at least nineteen of these excellent booklets published by Old Sturbridge, Inc., Sturbridge Village, Massachusetts. There is no finer reference material published today on the New England period 1790-1840. Among the booklets the author found helpful were: *Country Stores in New England*, Gerald Carson; *Architecture in Early New England*, Abbott Lowell Cummings; *New England Character and Characters As Seen by Contemporaries; The New England Village Scene: 1800, Textiles in New England, Town Schooling in Early New England*, Catherine Fennely; *Child Life in New England*, Elizabeth Speare; *Customs on the Table Top*, Helen Sprackling; *Food, Drink and Recipes of Early New England*, Jane Whitehill; *The Village Mill in Early New England*, Edward P. Hamilton.

The Prentis Collection. Concord: New Hampshire Historical Society, 1958.

Readable Books about Early American History. Williamsburg, Va.: Institute of Early American History and Culture, 1960.

Winship, Stephen W. *At the Bend in the River. Concord, New Hampshire, Bicentennial. 1765-1965*. Concord: Concord Bicentennial, Inc., 1965.

Index

Abbott, Elias, 88

Abolition, 35, 54, 94, 136

Academies, 90, 91, 100
   See also individual academies

Alcott, Bronson, 64

Ambrose, David (uncle), 56

Ambrose, Nathaniel (grandfather), 36, 56, 58, 173

Ambrose, Nathaniel (cousin), 58

Ambrose family, 20, 36

Ambrose Meeting House, 36

Avon, Mass. (Stoughton), 149, 154, 157

Baker, Aaron (cousin), 48, 64, 169

Baker, Abigail Ambrose (mother), 16-20, 28, 29, 34-39, 41, 49, 56, 64, 65, 71, 73, 83, 89, 107, 108, 118-120, 146

Baker, Abigail Barnard (Abby) (sister), 16, 19, 31, 33, 34, 50, 52, 69, 73-80 passim, 84-86, 100, 106, 110-113, 118-124, 127-130, 133, 138, 139, 151, 152, 178, 181

Baker, Albert (brother), 15, 16, 23, 30, 31, 45, 46, 50-52, 53-55, 61, 63, 66-71, 78, 82-85, 92, 99-101, 108, 151, 175
   career, 68, 69, 85, 94, 95, 98
   correspondence with George, 53, 68, 69, 72, 78, 84-86, 94

Baker, Amos (cousin), 97

Baker, Elizabeth Patterson (stepmother), 121, 124

Baker, George Sullivan (brother), 15, 16, 23, 31, 44, 50, 52, 66-73, 86, 88, 96-99, 103-106, 109-114 passim, 118, 119, 128, 130, 154, 180
   correspondence with Albert, 53, 68, 69, 72, 78, 85, 86, 94
   letters from home, 67, 68, 74-77, 80, 83, 84, 86, 120, 123, 124, 154, 155, 170, 171
   See also Baker family, letters quoted

Baker, Mrs. George S.; see Rand, Martha

Baker, Hannah Lovewell (great-grandmother), 25, 26, 35, 169

Baker, James (uncle), 19, 30, 169

Baker, Joseph (great-grandfather), 25, 28

Baker, Joseph (grandfather), 18, 26-28, 31, 40, 169, 171

Baker, Luke (cousin), 30

Baker, Mark (father), 7, 16, 17, 18-20, 28-38 passim, 40-46, 47, 48, 52, 56-59, 64, 65, 70, 71, 75-77, 79, 80, 81, 86, 87, 88, 89, 98, 100, 103-107, 110, 118, 120, 121, 124, 125, 141, 169, 171, 172, 173, 174
   See also Baker family

Baker, Martha Smith (sister), 16, 19, 23, 31-34, 50, 52, 73-80, 83-85, 88, 96, 98, 100-108 passim, 116, 117, 120, 123, 124, 127-130, 133

Baker, Maryann (grandmother), 16, 18, 23-32 passim, 41, 66, 170

Baker, Mary Ann (aunt), 20

Baker, Mary Morse; see Eddy, Mary Baker

Baker, Philip (uncle), 19, 20, 30, 32, 52, 70, 71, 97, 169

Baker, Samuel Dow (brother), 15, 16, 30, 50, 51, 54, 78, 85, 101, 106, 128

Baker, Thankful, 24

Baker, Thomas (emigrant), 24

Baker family, 8, 14, 15-22, 23, 26, 27, 28-31, 36-38, 41, 42, 52, 66-79 passim, 83, 85, 106, 111, 169, 178
   letters quoted, 67-86 passim, 98, 99, 117-129 passim

Baptist churches, 56, 57

Bartlett, John, 83, 101, 102, 110, 111, 115, 118, 119, 120, 182

Belknap Gazette, 94, 97, 180

Bodwell, Abraham, 77, 87, 100, 178, 179

Bodwell, Sarah, 77, 78, 90, 91, 93, 94, 100, 179, 180

Boswell, Rev. (Baptist minister), 57

Bouton, John Bell, 59, 60

Bouton, Nathaniel, 58, 59, 63, 70

Bow, N. H., 7, 8, 24-30, 33, 45, 56, 57, 68, 166
   Baker homestead in, 8, 14, 15, 18-20, 23, 26, 27, 66, 69-71, 169, 178

Bow Bog Meeting House, 56
Bow Center, N. H., 40, 56
Burnham, Abraham, 31, 52, 57, 65, 66, 176

Calvinism, 18, 63-65, 82, 87
Charleston, S. C., 100, 105-107
Cheney, Russell, 120
    See also Sanborn, Mahala
Christian Science, 147-156 passim
Christian Science Church, 162-164, 165
Christian Science Journal, The, 162
Christian Science Monitor, The, 164, 186
Christian Science Sentinel, 162
Clark, George, 146, 147
Clark, Jonas B., 142
Clement, Priscilla, 77, 178
Clement, Sarah, 111, 112
Concord, N. H., 7, 15, 16, 20, 30, 56, 58, 61, 67, 74,
    101, 166, 167
    Mrs. Eddy's home in, 13, 166
Congregationalist churches, 31, 36, 56-58, 62,
    63, 77, 80
Corser, Bartlett, 81, 82
Corser, Enoch, 80-83, 87, 90, 96, 100, 112, 181
Covenant, The, 112
Crafts, Hiram, 149, 150
Curtice, Corban, 106, 112, 113, 181

Dartmouth College, 31, 52, 53, 68, 78
Dow family (Concord, N. H.), 20
Duncan, Elizabeth Patterson (stepmother),
    121, 124
Dunstable, N. H., 24
Durgin, Hazen, 29
Durgin, Lyman, 89, 90, 96, 97

Eddy, Asa Gilbert, 161, 162

Eddy, Mary Baker, 13, 28, 29, 60-66, 70, 71, 77,
    87, 88, 102, 117, 136-140, 178
    anecdotes of, 33, 34, 39, 42, 46, 47, 49, 50, 52
    autobiography, 14, 157
    Bible study, 23, 37, 97, 114, 130, 131, 137-147
        passim, 152, 156, 159, 160
    birth and ancestry, 15-19, 23, 24
    birthplace, 7, 22, 23, 26, 166
    early travels, 95, 103-105, 109, 114
    education, 31-34, 42, 43, 46, 50-55, 68, 74, 77-93
        passim, 100, 101, 179
    health, 46, 48, 71, 83-85, 98-100, 104, 105, 109-
        115, 119, 120, 123-142 passim
    homes, 13, 127, 130, 133-136, 140, 141, 147,
        149, 151, 156, 158-161, 165-167, 186
    influence of Albert, 23, 50, 53-55, 78, 92,
        98, 108
    quotations from writings, 13, 15, 18, 24, 28,
        34, 40, 45, 50, 56, 57, 61, 66, 71, 79, 88, 94,
        100, 107, 116, 123, 130, 131, 133, 134, 138,
        143, 144, 146, 149-152, 155, 156, 160, 164,
        166, 168
    relationship to Christian Science: as Dis-
        coverer, 14, 141-145, 150-157 passim, 162,
        163, 164, 184
        as Founder and Leader, 13, 161-169
        as healer, 130, 134, 145, 147-149, 152-162
            passim, 166
        as lecturer, 155, 163
        as teacher, 90, 111, 112, 128, 147, 149, 150,
            155, 157, 159, 160, 162, 163
        as writer, 31, 54, 55, 93-99 passim, 106,
            108-114, 126, 133, 138, 140, 141, 155-162
            passim, 182
    See also Glover, Mary Baker; Patterson,
    Mary Baker
Education; see New England, education in
Emerson, Ralph Waldo, 63
"Emma Clinton," 114

First Congregational Church, Concord, N. H.
    see Old North Church
Floral Wreath, The, 108, 112

Franklin, N. H., 124, 125
Freemason's Monthly, 112
French and Indian War, 25, 26
Fuller, Margaret, 64

Gault, Andrew, Sr., 16, 19, 43, 52, 56
Gault, Andrew, Jr., 73, 95
Gault, Daniel, 73
Gault, Matthew, 33
Gault, Sarah (Sally) Knox, 16-18, 169
Glover, Andrew, 121, 122
Glover, Eliza Ann, 54
Glover, George Washington (husband), 54, 85, 100-109, 121, 146
Glover, George Washington (Georgy) (son), 107-129 *passim,* 136, 165, 183
Glover, Mary Baker, 106-109, 113, 120-125, 128, 129, 136, 146, 151, 165, 166
    See also Eddy, Mary Baker
Godey's Lady's Book, 93

Hall, Grace, 135
Hall, Nettie, 135
Haverhill, N. H., 101, 105
High schools, 90, 91, 100
Hill, N. H., 83, 137
Hillsborough, N. H., 44, 53, 55, 68, 69, 73, 83, 85, 94
Hillsborough Academy, 69
Hinds, Orlando, 57
Holmes, Augusta, 78, 87, 96, 98, 101, 102, 105, 139
Holmes, Nathaniel, 78, 98
Homeopathy, 132, 142, 144, 149, 183
Hooksett, N. H., 29
Huntoon, Mehitable, (cousin), 49
Hypnotism, 136, 137, 159
    See also Quimby, Phineas

Indian troubles, 24-26

Kidder, Daniel, 128

Lane, Caroline, 111
Loudon, N. H., 29, 80
Lovewell, John, 24-27
Lynn, Mass., 140, 158-161
Lynn Weekly Reporter, 140

McNeil, John, 24
Masons (Freemasons), 108, 109
Meeting House, White Rock Hill, 17, 27, 40, 41
Mental suggestion, 137, 144
Mesmerism, 137, 159
    See also Quimby, Phineas
Methodist churches, 56, 57, 102, 110
Murray, Lindley, 53, 54, 114, 176
Muster Day parade, 97

New England, 137
    education in, 30-33, 45, 46, 50, 79, 80, 90, 91, 100, 101, 128, 175, 176, 178
    industrial revolution in, 36, 70
    life in, 19, 22, 27
    religious environment in, 16, 17, 59-61, 63, 64
    transportation in, 15, 20, 21, 26, 95, 107, 153
New Hampshire Conference Seminary, 110, 111
New Hampshire Patriot, 112, 124
New York Evening Post, 93
Newhall, George, 141, 142
Northfield, N. H., 87, 88
North Groton, N. H., 120, 121, 127, 129, 130, 133

Odd Fellows, 112
Old North Church, Concord, N. H., 58-60, 62

191

Patterson, Daniel, 124-129, 133-141 *passim,* 146

Patterson, Mary Baker, 124-129, 133-141 *passim,* 146, 147, 151
   See also Eddy, Mary Baker

Pembroke, N. H., 7, 26, 31, 36, 56-58, 61, 62

Pembroke Academy, 30, 31, 52

Pembroke Sabbath School Society, 56

Phillips, Dorr, 147, 148

Phillips, Susan, 148, 149

Pierce, Benjamin, 44, 53

Pierce, Franklin, 45, 53, 55, 68, 69, 83, 98, 124, 136, 175

Pilsbury, Amos, 67

Pilsbury, Ellen (Nell) (niece), 108, 117, 120, 124, 139, 152-154, 183

Pilsbury, Luther, 101, 116, 120
   See also Baker, Martha S.

Pilsbury, Mary Neal (niece), 120, 124, 128

Pilsbury, Moses, 67

Pleasant View, Concord, N. H., 13, 166

Plymouth Academy, 180

Portland Advertiser, 138

Portland Courier, 138

Predestination, doctrine of, 63, 64

Protracted meetings; *see* Revivals

Public speaking, training in, 51, 93

Quimby, Phineas, 136-141, 183

Rand, Martha (Mathy), 101, 110, 111, 115-117, 119, 123, 129, 154

Red Rock, Lynn, 158

Retrospection and Introspection, 14, 15, 18, 24, 28, 34, 40, 45, 50, 56, 61, 66, 71, 79, 88, 94, 100, 107, 116, 123, 130, 138, 144, 150, 157

Revivals, 61-66, 102, 177

Rogers, Josiah, 71

Roxbury, Mass., 24

Rumney, N. H., 134-136

Rust, Richard, 111

Sanborn, Dyer H., 91, 100, 101, **175, 178-180**

Sanborn, Hannah, 101

Sanborn, Mahala, 110, 113, 120-122, 127-130

Sanbornton, N. H., 7, 66, 70, 71, 73, 80, 83, 86, 97, 102, 106, 113, 138
   See also Sanbornton Bridge; Sanbornton Square

Sanbornton Academy, 79, 81, 83, 100, 101, 110, 179

Sanbornton Bridge (Tilton), N. H., 70, 73, 74, 77, 79-81, 87, 100, 102, 118, 139
   See also Sanbornton

Sanbornton-Northfield church, 87, 88

Sanbornton Square, N. H., 73, 77, 79, 87, 90, 91, 97
   See also Sanbornton

Schools, 30, 33, 34, 45, 50, 77, 80, 90, 91, 100, 101
   See also Academies; New England, education in

Science and Health with Key to the Scriptures, 13, 150, 156, 158-161, 163

Science of Man," "The, 155

Slavery, Issue of, 35, 54, 94, 136

Smith, Hildreth H. (cousin), 82

Stoughton, Mass., 157
   See also Avon, Mass.

Sunday Schools, 56-58, 88, 161

Swampscott, Mass., 140, 141

Temperance lodge, 140, 141

Test of Love," "The, 114

Thoreau, Henry David, 64

Tilton, Albert (nephew), 110, 112, 113, 139

Tilton, Alexander, 78, 79, 86, 98, 111, 113, 115, 118, 127, 128, 138

Tilton (Mrs. Alexander), *see* Baker, Abigail

Tilton, Evelyn (niece), 139
Tilton, N. H., 7, 11, 70, 100
Tin Corner district school, 77, 101
Transcendentalism, 63, 64
Turner, Sarah, 130, 131

Union Church, Bow, N. H., 56
Universalism, 48

Water-cure, 137
Wentworth family, 157, 158
White, Daniel, family, 38
White Rock Hill, 17, 27, 40
Wilmington, N. C., 108
Wilson, Myra, 132, 133
Women and women's rights, 35, 50, 52, 182
Woodman (Woodman-Sanbornton) Academy, 77, 79, 90. 91, 97, 100, 111, 179

Copy #1

Date Due

9/11/67			
9/27/67			
7/19/68			
6/9/70			
8/4/70			
9/30/70			
1/10/72			
9/7/72			
11/16/73			
8/1/74			
5/30/75			

Library Bureau Cat. No. 1137